With thanks to

Dr Imogen Gibbon, Chief Curator and Deputy Director, Scottish National Portrait Gallery

Professor Gerry Carruthers, Co-Director, Centre for Robert Burns Studies, Glasgow University, and all staff

Mr C M McGibbon, Grand Secretary, Royal Order of Scotland

Mr Patrick J Givan, PM. Lodge Secretary, Lodge Canongate Kilwinning No.2

Nat Edwards, for his help when he was Director, Robert Burns Birthplace Museum, Alloway

Rebecca McCallum Stapley, Curator, Robert Burns Birthplace Museum, Alloway

Robert L Betteridge, Curator, Rare Books and Music Collections, National Library of Scotland

Manuscript Collections Division, National Library of Scotland

Special Collections Department, Mitchell Library, Glasgow

Phillip Hunt, Photography & Licensing Assistant, National Galleries of Scotland

Dt Joanna Soden, Collections Curator, Royal Scottish Academy

Denise Brace, Curator-History, The Museum of Edinburgh

Richard Hunter, Edinburgh City Archives

Mr Andrew Hamilton, Lodge St Andrews, Edinburgh

Lt Col Richard Callander OBE TD, Secretary QBGS, Royal Company of Archers

Leifur Breidfjord, Painter and Stained Glass Artist

Angus Gordon Lennox, Gordon Castle, Fochabers

Ros Lewis, Events and Business Development, Gordon Castle, Fochabers

Jesper Ericsson, Curator, The Gordon Highlanders Museum, St Luke's, Viewfield Road, Aberdeen
www.gordonhighlanders.com

The Hunter Foundation, Rab Wilson and Professor Caroline Wilkinson, Professor of Cranial Identification,
University of Dundee

Professor Arnold Myers, Edinburgh University Collection of Historical Musical Instruments

Matthew Whithey, Curator, The Abbotsford Trust, Abbotsford

David Medcalf, Photographer

Gordon Irving, Artist

Iain T Watt, Past President, Sandyford Burns Club

Marcin Klimek, Photo Librarian, The National Trust For Scotland

Kim Traynor, Photographer

Jason Sutcliffe, The Dick Institute, Kilmarnock

Dr Helen Marlborough

Professor David Purdie

Dr Ronnie Scott

Anne MacKinnon

Contents

Introduction	6
Political Background	11
Freemason's Hall	16
The Scottish National Portrait Gallery	20
What Did Robert Burns Really Look Like?	21
The Scottish National Portrait Gallery	24
John Flaxman	29
York Place and St James Square	30
Alexander Nasmyth	31
Sir Henry Raeburn	34
St James Square	36
Sylvander and Clarinda	40
John Beugo	43
William Cruikshank	44
Jean Cruikshank	44
The Jacobite Rebellions and Tartan	46
Theatre Royal	48
David Ross	50
John Home	51
William Woods	52
Walter Scott	53
Old Calton Burial Ground	54
Scottish American Memorial	58
Political Martyrs' Monument	60
David Hume	62
David Allan	64
14 Calton Hill	65
Agnes 'Nancy' McLehose – Clarinda	66
Professor Dugald Stewart	69
Burns Monument	72
Sir James Shaw, Baronet	74
Canongate	76
Kirk of the Canongate	77
Robert Fergusson	79
John Campbell	82
Reverend Robert Walker	83
St John Street	84

Lodge Canongate Kilwinning No. 2	86
James Cunningham	89
James Burnett – Lord Monboddo	92
Elizabeth (Bess) Burnett	93
Henry Erskine	94
James Tytler	95
Rev Bishop John Geddes	98
The Episcopal Chapel (St Patrick's Church)	99
Reverend Archibald Alison	100
St Cecilia's Hall (Museum of Instruments)	101
Girolamo Stabilini	103
Domenico Corri	103
Johann Georg Christoph Schetky	104
Peter Taylor	106
High Street	108
Carrubber's Close	109
Craig's Close	110
William Creech	111
Henry Mackenzie	114
Louis Cauvin	115
James Johnson	117
Anchor Close	119
Andrew Bell	121
William Smellie	122
St Giles' Cathedral	124
The Luckenbooths	127
William 'Deacon' Brodie	130
James Sibbald	132
John Kay	133
Lord William Craig	135
John McLaurin, Lord Dreghorn	136
Peter Hill	137
Peter Williamson, 'Indian Peter'	138
Lawnmarket	140
Wardrop's Court	141
Site of Baxter's Close	142
The Writers' Museum	144
Jean Lorimer	146
George Thomson	148
Allan Ramsay, Snr	150
Ramsay's House	151

White Hart Inn	152	Patrick Miller of Dalswinton	177
Greyfriars Kirkyard	155	General's Entry	179
		Robert Ainslie	180
George Square	156	Reverend John Kemp	181
George Square	157	Jenny Clow	183
The Douglas Cause	158	John Miers	184
Sir Walter Scott	160	Craufurd Tait	185
Assembly Rooms	163	Buccleuch Parish Church	186
Jane Maxwell Alexander, Duchess of Gordon	164	Alison Cockburn Rutherfurd	187
Buccleuch Pend	167	Dr Thomas Blacklock	188
William Nicol	167	Margaret Chalmers	191
Allan Masterton	169	After Edinburgh	193
Archers' Hall	170		
Sciennes Hill House	172	The Shaw Burns – Investigating a Painting	196
Rankeillor Street	174	Bibliography	200
Alexander Findlater	175	Online Resources	204
Nicolson Square	176	Image Credits	205

Poetry, Epitaphs

Birthday Ode for the 31st December 1787	39	Ye Jacobites By Name	118
Sylvander to Clarinda	42	On William Smellie	123
Epitaph for Mr W Cruikshank	44	On William Creech	128
A Rosebud by My Early Walk	45	Written under the Portrait of the Celebrated	
Such a Parcel Of Rogues In A Nation	47	Miss Burns	137
Prologue spoken by Mr Woods	53	Address to Edinburgh	143
To Messrs Muir, Palmer, Skirving and Margarot	61	Lassie wi' the lintwhite locks	147
To a Lady with a present of a pair		Ae Fond Kiss	154
of drinking glasses	68	Castle Gordon	166
Lines on Meeting with Lord Daer	71	Epitaph For William Nicol	168
Here Lies Robert Fergusson, Poet	81	Address to the Unco Guid	182
Lament for James, Earl of Glencairn	90	Epistle to Dr Blacklock	190
Elegy On The Late Miss Burnet Of Monboddo	93	My Peggy's Charms	192
Extempore in the Court of Session	94	My Luve is like a Red, Red Rose	195
Clarinda (Mistress of my soul)	105		
Lament For The Absence Of William Creech,			
Publisher	113		

Introduction

This book about Burns in Edinburgh is arranged, not in chronological order of his visits, but by district and area. Robert Burns made several significant visits to Edinburgh and this book has been designed for the reader to be able to absorb as many insights into Burns' time in the city as possible – to see those places which he visited that remain, and others which are important and relevant.

Above: Agnes Burnes

Robert Burns was born on 25th January 1759 in Alloway, two miles from the town of Ayr in the west of Scotland. He was born in the family home, a small clay and thatched-roof cottage built by his father, William Burnes.

William Burnes' early years are a little vague. His father Robert, the poet's grandfather, rented Clochnahill Farm on the Dunnottar estate of George Keith, 10th Earl Marischal. The role of the Marischal was to serve as custodian of the Royal Regalia of Scotland and to protect the king when he attended parliament. A Jacobite sympathiser, Keith was charged with treason for his part in the 1715 and 1719 risings forcing him to flee to the Continent where he continued to serve the Jacobite cause. His lands were confiscated by the Crown in 1720. Robert continued to work the farm but bad weather, low prices and the economic aftermath of the '45 rising forced him to give up the lease.

Many families were forced out of the Highlands and into the Lowlands in search of work and William Burnes eventually found himself in Edinburgh working on the newly formed Hope Park, now known as the Meadows, on the south side of the City. He worked there for two years as a landscape gardener before moving to the west coast of the country, to Fairlie in Ayrshire, where he had the offer of a job.

Below: Burns Cottage, Alloway

William settled in Alloway and married Agnes Broun (Scots spelling of Brown) on 15th December 1757. Robert was born on 25th January 1759 and Gilbert in 1760. There followed another two boys and three girls.

William, a very independently minded man, was deeply religious and believed that in order to make progress in the world his children should be able to read and write and have at least a basic education, so Robert (at age 6) and Gilbert (at age 5) were enrolled in Alloway School. When the school was forced to close due to financial pressures, William persuaded neighbours to hire John Murdoch from Ayr to teach the children.

Murdoch was 18 years old and had been educated in Edinburgh. Murdoch gave the boys the foundation of a classical education, teaching them the Bible, and exposing them to the works of Shakespeare, Milton, Dryden and the finest writers of the day.

When Murdoch left to take up another paying post in Dumfries, William continued to teach the boys himself and enrolled them in Dalrymple School, which they had to attend week about, because both could not be spared from farm work at the same time.

Below: Burns Cottage, (rear)

In 1773 John Murdoch returned to Ayr and Robert spent three weeks with him, studying English, French and Latin.

Robert was an avid reader from this time, and for the rest of his life. As a family they could be found in the evenings reading to their father, or each other. Robert, in one of his letters, remarked that he was inspired by the tales of Hannibal and of Sir William Wallace, *"who poured a Scottish prejudice into my veins which has boiled there in each and every one of my waking moments.",* so much so that as a boy he would imagine he was Wallace and marched alongside soldiers as they passed through the town.

In his later years Robert would have books delivered from France, regularly reading the original French versions. A partly read book, in French, was on his bedside table on the day he died.

Robert started writing verse when he was 15 years old. The reason? He had fallen in love with Nelly Kilpatrick. For the rest of his short life he was to fall in love regularly, expressing his thoughts and emotions in poems and songs.

Robert's early life was hard – very hard. It was a constant struggle to farm on poor soil and despite moving from farm to farm there was never any money to invest in more modern farming equipment resulting in the family continuing to live in near poverty. Despite this, Robert worked long hours and developed a slight stoop due to the time spent on the plough.

It was these long hours, and a poor diet from a very young age which did lasting damage to Burns' health. Damage that meant that despite his reputation, he would never be a heavy drinker as alcohol upset his already delicate stomach.

Above: Burns Cottage, (interior)

On the 4th July 1782, when he was 22 years old, Robert joined the Freemasons. This membership not only cemented friendships and relationships with people he already knew in his local area, but was an invaluable source of contact and introduction when he found himself in Edinburgh.

On 13th February 1784 his father William died at the age of 63. Robert was 25 years old and now found himself the head of a large family. His father had been fighting a legal battle over the farm and after several years he won the court case, but the years of toil and hardship had taken its toll on William. Robert simply had to work harder to keep the farm going since he was now the provider for his siblings and his mother.

It was around this time that the family name was changed from Burnes to Burns. There may have been a variety of reasons for this, one of them being that Burnes was a Kincardineshire name and Robert and Gilbert may have decided to change it to the Ayrshire form. It may also have been an attempt to avoid some of the people who had been pursuing them for money.

On 22nd May 1785, Elizabeth Paton (his mother's servant) gave birth to Robert's first child, also Elizabeth. Robert's mother took the child in and raised her as one of her own.

Jean Armour, whom he had first met at a dance in April of 1785, became pregnant. They did intend to marry but Jean's father, knowing of Robert's reputation, wanted his daughter to have nothing to do with him, sending Jean off to Paisley.

Robert had reached a turning point in his life. The farm was not going well, the Kirk was pursuing him as a fornicator and Robert felt that the world was conspiring against him.

Through his various contacts he was offered a job as a Plantation Manager in the West Indies, and decided to go to Jamaica. It was a drastic step but how could he raise the money for the trip?

Below: William Burns' gravestone, in Alloway Kirk

Some friends suggested that he publish some of his work to raise the money. Burns was well known in the area as a 'maker of rhymes' (in Scots the word for poet is 'makar') regularly writing out copies of his poems and giving them to friends and acquaintances; a practice he maintained all of his life, regularly enclosing new poems and songs along with letters to friends. It was common in those days for books to be published by subscription, so Burns began planning his book.

The only printing press in Ayrshire was located nearby in Kilmarnock. Its owner, John Wilson, an exact contemporary of Robert Burns, had already published an edition of Burns' beloved poet Milton in 1785. In April 1786 the subscription sheets were printed by Wilson, and Robert's fund-raising was complete when 13 fellow members of the Masonic Lodge pledged to take 350 of the 650 volumes to be printed.

Above: Gilbert Burns

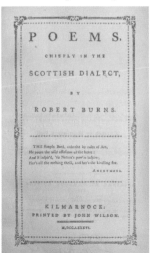

His fare to Jamaica was 9 guineas and publication of the book would surely raise that amount, but in the meantime Robert's troubles were building as he was making plans. On 23rd April, James Armour repudiated Robert as a son-in-law and Robert was also forced to repudiate Jean. On 13th June, Jean went before the Kirk and advised them that she was with child and Robert was the father. This started a furore against Robert yet again in the Kirk and he was ordered to make 3 public appearances as a fornicator, the first of which was on 25th June.

On 22nd July, Robert had a Deed of Assignment drawn up and lodged with the Sheriff-Clerk at Ayr.

Left inset: The title page of *Poems, Chiefly in The Scottish Dialect*

Above: Benjamin Franklin

Below: Statue of Jean Armour, Dumfries, erected by Dumfries Burns Howff Club in 2004

JEAN ARMOUR
1765 – 1834
WIFE OF ROBERT BURNS
ERECTED BY
BURNS HOWFF CLUB
SEPTEMBER 2004

This basically transferred all of Robert's assets to Gilbert, his share of the farm, all profits from the book and it also made Gilbert responsible for the upbringing of Robert's illegitimate daughter, Elizabeth.

However, on 30th July, James Armour took a writ out against Robert and, terrified of being arrested and thrown into prison, he went into hiding at his uncle's home near Kilmarnock.

As providence would have it, on the following day, 31st July 1786, his book, *Poems Chiefly in the Scottish Dialect*, went on sale and was an immediate success, selling over 600 copies and earning Robert more than enough for his trip to Jamaica.

Robert Burns was suddenly a successful writer who was being spoken of the length and breadth of Scotland.

Even when Jean gave birth to twins, Robert and Jean, (the Kirk stated that children born out of wedlock be named after the parents) on 3rd September, he still planned to go to Jamaica, but all that was to change with one message from Edinburgh.

A copy of the book had made its way into the hands of Dr Thomas Blacklock, known as The Blind Poet. Blacklock's poetry was much respected and he was acquainted with such famous figures as Dr Samuel Johnson and his biographer James Boswell, as well as the philosopher David Hume and one of the most famous Americans, Benjamin Franklin.

Indeed Blacklock was so full of praise for Burns' work that he advised him to come to Edinburgh immediately where a second, larger, edition could be published. He was sure it would have a more universal circulation than "*anything else that had been published within his memory*".

Burns had naturally been thinking of a second edition as the first had sold out so quickly, and being a prolific writer, he already had new material. John Ballantyne, an Ayrshire banker, offered to lend him money for the second edition; he also advised Burns to look for a publisher in Edinburgh.

So it was that on 27th November 1786 Robert Burns, on a pony borrowed from his friend George Reid, set off on the two-day trip to Edinburgh.

Reid had arranged for Burns to break his trip at Covington Mains Farm, by Biggar, and rest overnight before travelling on. Reid had also arranged for the farmers of the area to call and meet their new hero in person. The signal of Burns' arrival was a white sheet tied to a pitchfork placed on a cornstack and on Burns' arrival the house was soon filled. The evening became part of the morning and, after his farewells, Burns breakfasted at the next farm with another large party.

Following lunch at the Bank in Carnwath and, after saying his goodbyes to the assembled well wishers, he rode on to Edinburgh in the evening.

Political

Background

The Act of Union in 1603, and the Act of Union of Parliaments in 1707 saw power move from the kingdom of Scotland, with its own religious, political and cultural characteristics, to London.

The Stuarts ruled Scotland from 1371 until 1603. The last king of the Stuart Dynasty was King James VI of Scotland and I of England. With the death of Elizabeth I in 1603, the crowns of Scotland and England became one. James VI of Scotland became James I of England and opted to have his throne in London, marking the end of Scotland's sovereign independency. James gathered notable Scots around him in London and gradually, through distance and marriage, chiefs became removed from their clans and the clan system, which had shared land between the chief and his clan. Land was now tenanted by clansmen, not owned, and the chiefs were granted land rights through royal charters from the king, leaving the clansmen vulnerable.

The chiefs remained in control of their clans until 1707, when Scotland joined with England in a common British state. The Union was accomplished in spite of fierce opposition. Scotland suffered greatly under English hands, and after the failure of the Darien scheme, Scotland was financially vulnerable. The Darien Scheme was a plan for the Kingdom of Scotland to become a world trading nation by establishing a colony called 'Caledonia' on the Isthmus of Panama on the Gulf of Darien in the late 1690s. It was backed with around a quarter of the money circulating in Scotland at the time (£200,000) with almost everyone who had cash reserves taking shares in 'The Darien Company'. The scheme failed. The Scots who sailed from Leith on 26th July 1698 were attacked by the Spanish who believed that the Isthmus was

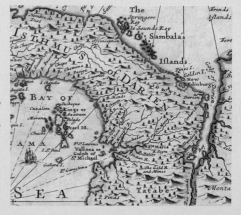

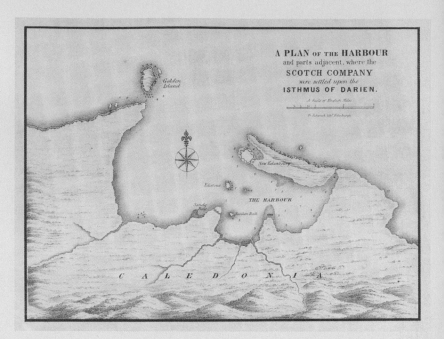

their territory. King William ordered the English in the West Indies and North America not to give any support. Scotland was on the brink of ruin. This was an important factor in weakening their resistance to the Act of Union.

It is also seen as marking a turning point – the beginning of the country's transformation into a business-oriented modern nation. The union with England seemed to offer a set of conditions where economic recovery might be achieved. The English and the Scots had become increasingly bitter towards each other, but this was the very reason why key statesmen on both sides of the border thought that the way to peace was to have one parliament governing both.

By now, England was trading with its West Indian and American colonies. The Act of Union allowed Scotland – particularly Glasgow – to also trade with the West Indies and America, especially in the tobacco and sugar businesses, which thrived. England became a market for Scots cattle-raisers and many new opportunities came to the fore. In this period the Scottish nation saw tremendous change and great hardship. Loyalties were divided and became confused between the Jacobite and Hanoverian causes. The Jacobites were a Catholic, political faction who supported the Stuart claim to the throne. The Jacobite name came from the Latin name for James (*jacobus*). They wished James II to be restored to the throne. The Hanoverians were so named because they supported the House of Hanover, and came to power in unsettling times that looked likely to threaten the stability of Britain. The first of their kings was George I, who was 52nd in line to the throne, but the nearest Protestant according to the Act of Settlement.

By the late 1700s, newspapers were being established, and gaining in circulation, and as the use of English and literacy was spreading in Scotland, Burns' volume of traditional Scottish songs was an instant success, which proved the loyalty people felt for the passing ways, and the oral tradition of recording culture. The growth of printing presses and printed material also meant that while local poets previously would have circulated pamphlets to readers within their circle, a wider

distribution of creative work was now possible. While the industrial revolution was just around the corner, change was apace. Farming was also revolutionising with the arrival of new machinery, and the new thinking on crop circulation and the management of livestock meant that the traditional method of farming in Scotland was disappearing. The smaller farmer, who in Scotland relied on the European runrig system, where strips of land were farmed and re-divided among the sharers, found survival hard. New crops (turnips/swedes) were introduced in the 18th century and the farming changes meant the end of the enclosure. The Clearances were still to come, but at this time, poor people had begun to be cleared from their homes to make way for grazing land for sheep. Previously sheep had been kept enclosed.

Small farmers such as Robert Burns' father, who relied on the plough, struggled. As a result families broke up, and people began to leave the land for cities, which grew rapidly.

By 1745 the Act of Union had been widely accepted in Scotland as a whole. The Lowlands enjoyed new prosperity as a result of the Scots being admitted to trade with the American colonies, and the west coast ports, particularly Glasgow, enjoyed a time of unprecedented commercial riches. The tobacco trade with the West Indies boomed until the American War of Independence, and while the sales of the once important linen industry fell, cotton mills took over the trade, as they were established in Renfrewshire and Lanarkshire.

After the 1745 Rebellion many defeated Scots Jacobites fled the country to the plantations in the American South, and to the West Indies to become slave masters. Robert Burns was one of many tempted by the prospects on offer, almost emigrating to Jamaica in 1786.

In 1762 Highland landlords introduced sheep to the hills and glens which offered greater profits than could be generated from tenant farmers. Later in the 18th century and well into the 19th century, Highland estates moved from arable and mixed farming. Surplus tenants were 'cleared' off the estates from about 1780.

Society also changed with the constraints brought by the establishment of the Kirk of Scotland (Presbyterian) in 1688. New schools, however poor, plus the growth of printing, and the changes to farming brought new ways to live. Singing, and telling stories – the oral methods by which we used to record our history – were disappearing. Burns' quest to collect traditional songs was timely, and he captured what we today think of as part of the Scottish traditional cultural identity. With all the changes in society then, one can see why his free expression and vitality was so important, and enjoyed.

Courtship, dalliance, legends, bawdy verse, poems and songs, love and drink, superstition and folk tales, told with humour, are captured in poems put to music by the young handsome farmer-poet around Edinburgh at a growing time of change throughout the UK.

The second half of the 18th century saw Scotland share in the wide cultural revolution which was happening all over Europe and many of the ideas and advances that emerged from the Scottish Enlightenment helped not only to reassert a Scottish identity, but contributed to shaping the modern world.

Scottish inventors were prominent at this time of great progress. James Watt patented the steam engine (1769) and the Scots led steam navigation. But with that said, there remained Jacobite sentiment and feeling and tension because of political change.

This period, often described as Scotland's Golden Age was an intellectual movement that ranged across the fields of science, industry, economics, culture, the law, engineering and medicine. All these areas saw major significant study and development as the great thinkers of the day grappled to understand and challenge the natural world and the human mind.

Enlightenment figures such as Robert Adam, James Hutton, David Hume, Joseph Black, James Watt, Adam Smith and Alison Rutherfurd urged people to think for themselves and speak out.

The Edinburgh that Burns discovered in 1786 reflected the failure of the

Jacobite rebellion of 1745–46, a turning point in Scottish history, and with the building work of The Southside and The New Town, Scotland's architects, builders, designers and traders were grasping new opportunities.

Burns arrived in Edinburgh during the evening of the 28th November 1786, unrecognised and headed for Baxter's Close, Lawnmarket, where he was welcomed by John Richmond, once a clerk with Burns' Ayrshire friend Gavin Hamilton.

Today Burns is seen as both the national poet of Scotland, and as a pre-Romantic poet. As much as he is valued for writing in the Scottish literary heritage, in the same traditional way as Scots vernacular writers Robert Henryson, William Dunbar, Allan Ramsay and Robert Fergusson, Burns is unique for expressing views that reflected the cultural and political changes in 18th century Scotland. Burns is valued for his spontaneity, his ability with language and the creation of phrases, his individualism, his gifted sensitivity and response to nature, his passion, his appreciation of rhyme and verse and his ability to express his thoughts in a memorable and inspirational way, as well as for what he was expressing – his strong arguments for freedom and his views against authority.

Burns wrote and created verse that captured a timeless universality that speaks to us today. His poor and rural birth meant he is viewed as speaking for the hardworking, honest and poor man with a vision of a free, better world. Burns is popular outside Scotland, particularly in Russia and China for these qualities.

Below: Leith Harbour, about 1700

Freemason's Hall

96 George Street, EH2 3HD

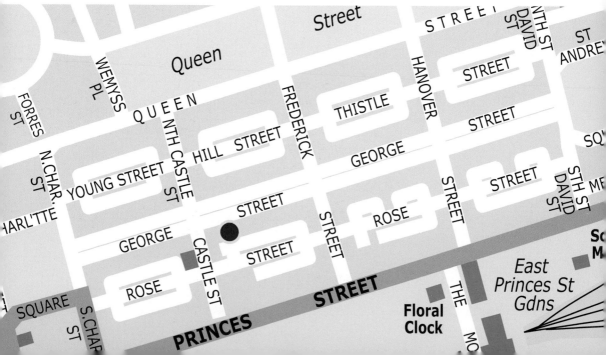

The museum holds several items associated with Burns, confirming the importance Freemasonry played in his life, none more so than the famous painting of his Inauguration as Poet Laureate of Scotland.

On the 4th July 1781 at the age of 22, Robert Burns was initiated as an Entered Apprentice Member of Lodge St David Tarbolton No. 174 and was to be an active member of the Masonic Order for the rest of his life.

At a meeting of Lodge Canongate Kilwinning No. 2 in Edinburgh on Thursday 1st February 1787, Robert Burns was made a member of the Lodge, the minutes of the meeting record the event. An increase in membership was noted; some were becoming masons in order to meet Burns.

Tradition has it that Burns was installed as Poet Laureate of the Lodge at a meeting on Thursday 1st March 1787. According to the painting which can be viewed in the Freemasons' Hall Museum, this was a huge occasion with 60 members identifiable in the painting. This depicted meeting, attended by the Grand Master Mason and all, does not appear in minutes, giving rise to the assumption, and no small amount of controversy, that it did not take place at all.

Lodge Canongate Kilwinning No. 2 have gone to some lengths to examine the case that, despite the absence of written proof, the Inauguration as depicted in the painting did take place. These points can be found on their Canongate Kilwinning website.

An exhaustive investigation was carried out by Hugh Peacock, secretary to the lodge from 1872 to 1873. Peacock mentions a meeting by Burns and the Reverend James Donald just a few months before Burns' death. At this meeting Burns gave details of being "*chosen poet laureate to a Meeting of Jacobite Gentlemen once in Edinburgh*".

The next written reference to Burns came when a resolution was passed at a meeting on the 8th June 1815, and recorded in the Minutes of the Lodge, authorising a subscription for a Mausoleum to Robert Burns, who is described

Above: The Inauguration of Robert Burns as Poet Laureate of Lodge Canongate Kilwinning No. 2, 1st March 1787, by William Stewart Watson, 1846

therein as one *"who had been Poet Laureate of the Lodge"*.

On that very day, 8th June 1815, 19 years after his death, the body of Robert Burns was transferred from his original grave in the corner of St Michael's Churchyard, Dumfries to the new Mausoleum in the church grounds.

What is on record is that on 13th January 1787 the Grand Master Mason of Scotland, Bro. the Hon. Francis Charteris paid his annual visit to Lodge St Andrew, Edinburgh.

At this time Lodge St Andrew had no permanent home, and so used various places in the old town, including St Mary's Chapel in Niddry Wynd, Blackfriars Wynd, Sheriff Clerk's Office in Brodie's Close, the Regent Hotel and Freemason Hall. However for the grand occasion of the visit of the Grand Master Mason of Scotland and Grand Lodge, the premises and Chapel of Lodge Canongate Kilwinning No. 2 in St John Street were used.

All of the Grand Lodge of Scotland was present, all of the different lodges of Edinburgh being represented, in all their pomp. As reported by the lodge, *"Sitting in the body of the Lodge amongst the other Visiting Brethren, is one of the greatest men and Masons who ever lived. He is 28 years of age! He is plainly, but properly dressed in a style midway between that of the holiday dress of a farmer and that of the company with which he is now associated. His shoulders are bent in the characteristic stoop of the ploughman. His face is turned towards the dais! He is all attention, for is not the Grand Master Mason proposing the toast of his health? The toast is: "Caledonia, and Caledonia's Bard, Bro. Robert Burns!"*

Burns records in a letter to John Ballantyne on the 14th January 1787, *"that he had no idea it would happen and was thunderstruck, trembling in every nerve"*.

Minutes of meetings at many Lodges were erratic, sometimes missing several weeks at a time, and Lodge St Andrew was no exception, minutes not being made for this particular occasion. Burns himself refers to the meeting as *'yesternight'*, causing yet more controversy of the exact evening. However it happened, Robert Burns was indeed looked upon as Poet Laureate of the Lodge.

The Inauguration was painted by William Stewart Watson in 1846, almost 60 years after the event.

Watson had been Depute Master of the Ancient Lodge of Edinburgh Mary's Chapel and had travelled to live and study in Rome, possibly also to escape the ravages of the cholera epidemic of 1832 which was sweeping through the city. On 26th November 1845 Watson was re-introduced as a member of the lodge after many years abroad by member James Marshall and it was Marshall who suggested that to demonstrate the artist's improved talents, he should carry out a painting of the Inauguration of Robert Burns as Poet Laureate of this lodge.

James Marshall offered to pay for the commission in return for the rights to sell engravings of the completed work.

Watson researched the event extensively, having access to lodge records and talking with older members to establish who would have been present. He then visited family and friends of those identified to find existing images and family records that he could use to produce portraits of those supposedly present. Remarkably, each and every one of those depicted is readily identifiable.

On completion of the painting, it was possible to purchase 28×18 inch engravings of the portrait from only £2.2s or, from a limited edition of 50, on India paper for £5.5s.

Above: Francis Charteris

Inauguration of Robert Burns as Poet Laureate of Lodge Canongate Kilwinning, No. 2, 1ˢᵗ March 1787 is a remarkable piece of social history of the day. It is a who's who of Edinburgh in the 1780s, lords and earls, landowners and bankers, actors and musicians, surgeons and advocates, teachers and publishers – no level of society is absent and all of those depicted had a direct connection with Robert Burns when he was in Edinburgh.

The National Museum of Scotland holds another version of the painting, *The Inauguration of Robert Burns as Poet Laureate of the Lodge*, which is most likely a working model used by Watson to plan a layout of the assembly. This painting, currently in the National Museum's storage facility, shows most of those in the main body of the room with those on the periphery of the portrait still to be added.

Also in the Freemasons' Hall museum are some items associated with Burns' membership from Dumfries including the Minute Book of Lodge St Andrews containing Robert Burns' signature and The Lodge Maul (mace).

There is also an engraving by Charles Ewart depicting Burns wearing a Masonic apron which is identical to the apron that Burns did wear. This very same Masonic Apron is on display, the material having been stabilised and preserved.

Freemason's Hall
96 George Street
EH2 3DH
0131 225 5577
curator@grandlodgescotland.org
www.grandlodgescotland.com

Below: The Inauguration of Robert Burns as Poet Laureate of the Lodge by William Stewart Watson, 1846

The Scottish National Portrait Gallery

1 Queen Street, EH2 1JD

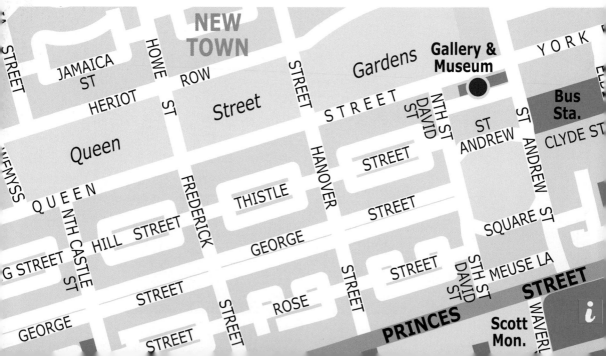

What Did Robert Burns Really Look Like?

D ebate, and a little controversy, has surrounded Burns' image. The Nasmyth painting of Burns shows an exceptionally handsome man, but was this the real Robert Burns?

Nasmyth's Burns, created for the frontispiece of the *Edinburgh Edition* of his book, and paid for by the publisher, was criticised on several occasions by people who actually knew Burns.

Now you can decide for yourself, as all of the portraits can be viewed at locations detailed within this book.

It is also worth noting that no established portrait painter ever painted Robert Burns, and this may be one of the reasons why likenesses vary. Even though Robert knew many of the artists of the day, in the aftermath of the Jacobite uprisings it was perhaps not entirely prudent for an established society portrait painter to have a radical like Burns sit for them as further commissions would likely disappear.

This did indeed happen to Alexander Nasmyth, a man of outspoken liberal views who was obliged to turn to landscape painting when commissions dried up.

Alexander Nasmyth's portrait of Burns, as mentioned above, was commissioned by William Creech the publisher, to be used as a frontispiece for the *Edinburgh Edition* of Burns' *Poems Chiefly in the Scottish Dialect*. It was the only recorded image of Robert Burns available until some 20 years after his death and is the image used and copied worldwide, during his lifetime and even now, more than 250 years later.

Above: Robert Burns (after Nasmyth)

As a young man Burns took great pride in his appearance. Always having an eye for the ladies, he dressed to stand out from the ordinary, and with saffron plaid and buckled shoes he certainly achieved that. The young Robert Burns couldn't be ignored, and being the first in his village to wear his hair tied back in a ponytail, ensured attention.

In *The Life of Robert Burns* (1886) by the Reverend George Gilfillan, we learn that Burns "*dressed like a farmer who had put on his best to dine with his laird*". He would be a very unusual farmer, with his wide-brimmed hat, topcoat and matching striped waistcoat.

Gilfillan continues that "*his best was a suit of blue and buff – the colours of the Whig party – with buckskin breeches and top boots*".

Burns was a striking and handsomely rugged figure. In his prime he was a sturdily built man with considerable strength from working at the plough, carrying sacks of meal and corn and from general farm work. At five feet ten inches tall, when he wore the wide-brimmed hat as was his custom, Burns would have been well over six feet tall, a very imposing figure indeed. He would certainly tower over the women of that time, many of whom would have been almost elfin-like in comparison.

Above:

(left) – Burns after Reid;

(middle) – in the style of Miers;

(right) – Reid/Miers montage

He had a slight stoop from his years at the plough, although it is recorded that when reciting poetry or engaged in debate his stature changed, the stoop disappeared, he stood upright and his manner was charming and dazzling.

Sir Walter Scott says of his eyes: "*His eyes were large, dark, and lustrous; I have heard them likened to coach lamps approaching in a dark night, because they were the first seen of any part of the poet. I never saw such another eye in a human head, though I have seen the most distinguished men of my time.*"

Robert Burns certainly had an almost magnetic presence about him. With charm in abundance and "*raven locks inclining to curl, a firm and manly mouth with bright white and regular teeth, and a dimple – a small one – on his chin*" it is little wonder women were attracted to him.

In 2013 Ayr artist Gordon Irving painted a portrait of Burns using a photograph of Jean Armour Burns Brown for reference. Jean Armour Burns Brown was Robert Burns' great granddaughter who was said to bear an uncanny resemblance to the poet.

Using photographic software to superimpose Jean's face, Irving then painted the portrait.

In 2013, state of the art forensic technology was used by Professor Caroline Wilkinson and her team at Dundee University to create an accurate 3D depiction of Burns' head.

This work referenced the Reid miniature and Miers silhouette, as well as facial measurements from other portraits.

A cast had been taken of Burns' skull when he was being re-interred in the new Burns Mausoleum at Dumfries; this was also available for those working on the project.

Rather than make our ideas of Burns' image clearer, Gordon Irving's artistic interpretation versus Dundee University's scientific reconstruction has managed to create even more discussion. Burns would have no doubt enjoyed that.

Far left: Gordon Irving's artistic interpretation

Left: Forensic Reconstruction by Professor Caroline Wilkinson

The Scottish National Portrait Gallery

Displaying many images of Burns, his friends and his acquaintances, including miniatures of the poet and his Clarinda – these are among the many fascinating items to be found in this wonderful building.

The Scottish National Portrait Gallery was designed by architect Sir Robert Anderson. When it opened in 1889 it was the first purpose-built portrait gallery in the world and today is home to Scotland's national collection of portraits.

Re-opened in 2012 after a two-year refurbishment programme, the Scottish National Portrait Gallery holds the 6 important images of Robert Burns in its collection including the original iconic Nasmyth image. Two of these pieces, both versions of the Taylor portrait, are on long-term loan, one being in The Writers' Museum and the other, at the time of writing, in St Cecilia's Hall.

The gallery is also home to images of many of the important people who were his friends and acquaintances while he was in Edinburgh. There are also paintings and early photographs of Burns' family and relations, as well as the famous Flaxman statue of Burns.

In the bright, cheerful café on the ground floor, you will find touchscreen displays. Included in *Faces and Places, Portraits of Scotland* is a Burns section which contains 16 images associated with him, from the painting by John Alexander Gilfillan (1822) of Jean Armour, to a photo by Brian Feinstein (1966, printed 2011) of Bob Dylan.

Dylan remarked more than once that Burns' poetry was a great inspiration, especially *Red, Red Rose.*

The gallery also houses the National Photography Collection.

GROUND FLOOR

On entering the building through the splendid main door on Queen Street, guarded by Sir William Wallace on one side and Robert the Bruce on the other,

Below: Scottish National Portrait Gallery

go through another set of doors and you will find yourself in the stunning main hall confronted by the white marble statue of Robert Burns by John Flaxman (begun in 1824) and surrounded above by the restored frieze of famous Scots through time.

The statue is flanked on either side by busts of Edinburgh's famous writers, Sir Walter Scott and Robert Louis Stevenson.

The Flaxman statue was removed from the Burns Monument in Regent Road in 1846 due to emissions from a nearby gasworks. It was first sent to The University of Edinburgh Library, then to the National Gallery of Scotland (now called the Scottish National Gallery) in 1861 before coming to its present home in 1889.

FIRST FLOOR

On the first floor, make your way to the library. There, on the right-hand side, under the cabinet entitled Portrait Medallions by James Tassie, you will see a set of drawers. Pull open the top drawer to find The Reid Miniature of Burns and the Miers Silhouette of Agnes McLehose, or Clarinda as she was known. Having been separated for over 225 years, Robert Burns and his Clarinda now sit facing each other.

As well as protecting the work from light, the drawers enable us to be very close to the work and see the very fine detail, even down to Clarinda's eyelashes. After two centuries, this is a remarkable testament to the quality of Miers' work.

This silhouette was made by John Miers in February 1788 at the request of Burns and this copy was apparently in Burns' possession at the time of his death.

Please examine all of the display drawers, where you will also find excellent miniatures of Jane, Duchess of Gordon and Alexander Runciman.

The miniature of Burns by Alexander Reid was painted after Burns had settled in Dumfries in 1795. Reid was a local miniaturist and Burns said of Reid's portrait in a letter to Mrs Riddell, *"I am just sitting to Reid in this town for a miniature, and I think he has hit by far the best likeness of me ever was taken."* In reality, just how accurate this was is open to debate as this was Burns' last year of life and he was already quite ill at this time.

This miniature was 'lost' until being rediscovered in 1885, meaning the Nasmyth portrait was the only available image of Burns for at least 20 years after his death and would perhaps explain its widespread use for everything to do with Robert Burns.

The second Nasmyth full-length portrait was executed in 1828, many years after the death of the poet. At the time of writing it is not included in any of the current exhibitions but can be viewed in the *Touchscreen Gallery: Faces & Places.* This again shows a slightly different interpretation of Burns probably due to the passing of time but also possibly influenced by the emergence of the Taylor portrait after 1812.

Above, left: Mrs Agnes McLehose, Clarinda, by John Miers
Above: Robert Burns by Alexander Reid

SECOND FLOOR

On the second floor, Gallery 7, in the *Age of Improvement* exhibition room, you will find a number of exceptional pieces associated with Burns. The Gallery Guides located at the entrance to each gallery are very useful large-print labels, each containing the same information as found on the wall labels beside each item.

In pride of place near the entrance is the world famous portrait by Alexander Nasmyth. It was commissioned by the publisher of the *Edinburgh Edition*,

Top: Alexander Nasmyth c1770s, from a self-portrait

Right: Robert Burns, 1759–1796. Poet by Alexander Nasmyth

Robert Burns

Engraved from a drawing of A.Nanning by C.Beugo

William Creech, in 1787 to be used as a design to illustrate the new publication. This may explain the romanticised image, but it should be noted that this was a commission which Nasmyth carried out for no fee – a gesture that Creech would be very happy with, as he was notoriously mean.

Left, inset: engraving after Nasmyth, by John Beugo

It was thought that after the death of Robert the painting was presented to Jean by Creech or even Nasmyth himself, however, in the *Works of Robert Burns; With His Life, Vol 6* by Allan Cunningham, the author asserts that *"This painting passed into the hands of Mrs Burns, after the death of Alexander Cunningham."* Alexander Cunnigham (1763–1814) was a writer to the Signet with chambers in St James Square, close to where Burns stayed with William Cruikshank. It is likely that they met in the square or at the Crochallan Fencibles club. Burns and Cunningham became regular correspondents throughout the poet's life, and Burns regarded him highly. Burns sent the first proof of *Tam O' Shanter* to Cunningham.

Further confusion is added by a letter from James Glencairn Burns to Burns' brother, Gilbert, when he writes that *"this picture was a very long time after my father's death in Edinburgh, first in the possession of Alexander Cunningham and afterwards of Mr Geo. Thomson."* However it would seem that the painting was eventually presented to Jean Armour Burns and thereafter bequeathed to Burns' son, Colonel William Nicol Burns, who in turn bequeathed it to the Scottish National Gallery. There are two Nasmyth sketches in The Portrait Gallery collection, available to be viewed by appointment, drawings made when walking with Burns in the countryside.

There are three further copies painted by Nasmyth, one of which hangs in the National Portrait Gallery, London, while another is in Kelvingrove Art Gallery and Museum, Glasgow.

A third, and previously unknown copy, was discovered in 2011 and after a two-year examination was authenticated in 2013. Thought to have been in the possession of Sir James Shaw in London, the portrait is known as the Shaw Burns and is currently in private ownership.

Burns and Nasmyth became very close friends and in a letter to the engraver John Beugo, Burns wrote, *"If you see Mr Nasmyth, remember me to him most*

respectfully, as he both loves and deserves respect; tho' if he would pay less respect to the mere Carcase of Greatness, I should think him much nearer perfection."

Nasmyth didn't fully complete the portrait, stopping at a point when he feared that he might spoil the end result. The canvas was then handed over to Beugo to make a copperplate engraving. Burns sat for Beugo several times and they also became close friends, even attending French classes together.

Also in this *Age of Improvement* room are several portraits of contemporaries of Burns.

Burns' publisher, William Creech, is represented in a magnificent painting by Sir Henry Raeburn (1806). Creech is famous for many reasons, among them his commissioning Nasmyth and Beugo to carry out the famous portrait of Burns. Creech also served on the jury at the trial of the infamous Deacon Brodie (portrayed in 1997 by Billy Connolly in a BBC film). Creech was also a bailie (a Scottish magistrate). [If you have time to visit the Bailie Bar, 2–4 St Stephen Street, you will see posters mentioning Creech and other bailies].

It was Dr John Moore (this painting is by Sir Thomas Lawrence c1790) to whom Burns wrote many letters including the well known autobiographical letter written while Burns was recovering from injury in August 1787.

Of great importance is the portrait of Professor Adam Ferguson. This very painting was on display in the house where Burns met the young Walter Scott.

Lifting the covers of the cases in the centre of the room, you will find, shielded from the sunlight, a collection of engravings by John Kay, who lived in 231 High Street, and made many remarkable likenesses of his contemporaries. James Burnett, Lord Monboddo is here. You will also be able to see Deacon Brodie, councillor by day and burglar by night, whose dual character is said to have influenced Robert Louis Stevenson's *Dr Jekyll and Mr Hyde*. There is also a self-portrait of Kay.

The room contains an impressive portrait of James Hogg, author of the magnificent *Confessions of a Justified Sinner*, and second Poet Laureate of Lodge Canongate Kilwinning No. 2 after Burns. There are also busts of Sir Walter Scott and Sir Henry Raeburn.

We can but touch upon the gems contained in this building – their own guide book runs to 224 pages!

Above: Henry Raeburn

Below: James Hogg

Scottish National Portrait Gallery
1 Queen Street
Edinburgh
EH2 1JD
0131 624 6200
pginfo@nationalgalleries.org
www.nationalgalleries.org/portraitgallery
Opening Hours:
Daily: Mon–Sun 10.00–17.00
Thur: 10.00–19.00

John Flaxman
1755–1826 Sculptor of Burns Statue

John Flaxman was born in York in 1755. His mother died when he was 9 years old and he was largely self-educated, first working at his father's plastercasting studio in London. He learned to draw and model from his father's stock and receiving gifts of books and advice, and later, commissions from his father's customers.

From the age of 12 he exhibited his work, regularly winning prizes through his teenage years, but was unable to obtain regular income. When he was 19 he began working for the Wedgwood Company – a position he held for the next 12 years, excelling not only as a modeller but also finding work as a monumental sculptor of grave monuments.

In 1782 he married Anne Denman and five years later they went to Italy where they stayed for 7 years where he directed the work of modellers employed by Wedgwood.

On their return they stayed in Fitzroy Square, London, where he continued to receive commissions for the rest of his life. In 1810 the position of chair of Sculpture at the Royal Academy was created especially for him.

Above: John Flaxman

His work in Scotland includes a bronze statue of Sir John Moore in Glasgow's George Square, the first statue erected in the square.

In 1824, Flaxman, then the leading sculptor of the Neoclassical movement in Britain, was commissioned to produce a life-sized model of Burns in marble, using the Nasmyth portrait as reference.

John Flaxman died suddenly on 3rd December 1826, aged 71. His brother-in-law, Mr Thomas Denman, completed the work in 1831.

Left, inset: Robert Burns statue by John Flaxman (for the Edinburgh Burns Monument), Scottish National Portrait Gallery

York Place and St James Square

❶ York Place

❷ Site of St James Square

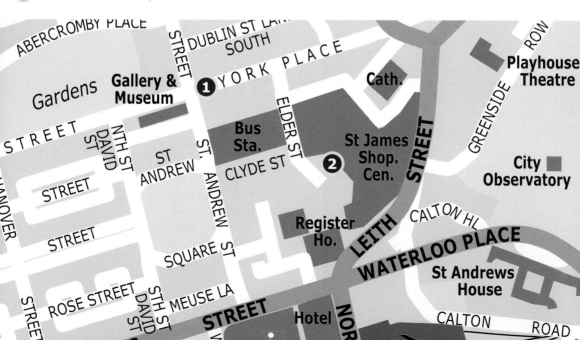

Alexander Nasmyth
1758–1840 Portrait Painter
47 York Place, EH1 3JD

The house and studio of Alexander Nasmyth who painted the iconic Burns portrait, and who became a close friend of the poet. It was here that Nasmyth painted the three copies of his portrait of Burns.

This house was designed and lived in by Alexander Nasmyth.

Nasmyth began his artistic career as an apprentice heraldic painter to a coachbuilder. His work impressed Allan Ramsay who took the young Nasmyth to London where he worked on subordinate portions of Ramsay's works. He returned to Edinburgh in 1778 becoming quickly established as a portrait painter. At this time he also assisted Patrick Miller of Dalswinton, as a draughtsman in his many mechanical researches and experiments.

In 1782, sponsored by Miller, Nasmyth left for Italy where he studied for two years.

Above: Alexander Nasmyth c1820s

On his return he found that his widely known liberal opinions gave offence to many of his aristocratic patrons; fewer commissions for portraits forced a move to landscape painting. During this period he also carried out scene-painting for theatre, including the Theatre Royals, Edinburgh, Glasgow and Dumfries.

Left: 47 York Place

The first of this esteemed artist's portraits of Robert Burns was commissioned by William Creech in 1787 to be engraved and used as the frontispiece for the *Edinburgh Edition* of Burns' *Poems Chiefly in the Scottish Dialect*. Creech invited Nasmyth to meet Burns, and the poet sat for the artist in Wardrop's Court.

In 1788, with Patrick Miller, Nasmyth designed a twin-hull iron boat propelled by steam-driven paddles. The boat was built by William Symington and tested on the 14th October 1788 on Dalswinton Loch, near Dumfries.

Burns visited Nasmyth half-a-dozen times for the portrait, and the pair became close friends, having similar political views. It was not unusual for them to walk in the countryside surrounding Edinburgh. On one celebrated occasion, after a long night in a High Street tavern, they walked the seven miles to Roslin, made famous recently by the book and film, *The Da Vinci Code*.

Below: Patrick Miller

Nasmyth's son, James, recalls the walk to Roslin in his autobiography: "*My father was so much impressed with the scene that, while Burns was standing under the arch, he took out his pencil and paper, and made a hasty sketch of the subject.*" This became the basis for Nasmyth's full length portrait in which he placed Burns in front of the Auld Brig o' Doon at Alloway.

Naysmith's artistic flair attracted the attention of landowners throughout the country and he was regularly employed to improve and beautify their country estates. With his knowledge of engineering and architecture he soon gained a deserved reputation. One of his better known projects was the design of the graceful temple covering St Bernard's Well by the Water of Leith, Stockbridge, Edinburgh.

For many years he ran a painting school at York Place, assisted by his daughters, teaching both amateur and professional painters. David Wilkie was among his celebrated pupils and it is thought that he taught James Ruskin, father of John Ruskin. It is likely that he set up the school in York Place around 1798.

The original Nasmyth portrait of Burns and a further two copies, all painted from life, would have been painted in Wardrop's Court. One of these, a previously unknown copy, was discovered at a sale in England in 2011. After a 2-year period of examination by various experts and being subjected to infrared and X-ray scrutiny, the painting was authenticated by David Mackie of Cambridge University, a leading academic in 18th-century Scottish painters. This copy is the only one of the four Nasmyth's retaining the original frame and glass and is likely to be the first of the copies, estimated as being painted around 1800 (see appendix for more details).

Known as the Shaw Burns, after Kilmarnock-born Sir James Shaw who is thought to have been the recipient of the painting, it is the only one of Burns by an artist he sat for that is in public hands.

A fourth copy, owned by George Thomson and currently in the National Portrait Gallery, London, would most likely have been painted in York Place.

After his death Nasmyth was described by Sir David Wilkie as "*the founder of the landscape painting school of Scotland*".

Alexander Nasmyth died in Edinburgh on the 10th April 1840, aged 82 and is buried in St Cuthbert's Churchyard at the west end of Princes Street.

Just four weeks after his death, *The Caledonian Mercury* reported that finished pictures from his studio, including some by Patrick and other members of the family, were sold at auction in Edinburgh as the family made arrangements to move to Manchester.

Opposite: Robert Burns by Alexander Nasmyth: 'The Shaw Burns'

Sir Henry Raeburn
1756–1823 Portrait Painter
Raeburn House
32 York Place, EH1 3HU

Below: 32 York Place. Raeburn House

Henry Raeburn was Scotland's leading portrait painter for over 30 years; he received his knighthood in 1822 when King George IV visited Edinburgh.

Born in the village of Stockbridge, now part of Edinburgh, Raeburn was orphaned in childhood, and raised in Heriot's Hospital where he was educated. At 15 years old he was apprenticed to a jeweller where he made various small pieces adorned with minute drawings on ivory, many of which still exist. It was a natural progression that he should turn to portrait miniatures, and subsequently oil painting, at which he was self-taught.

In his early 20s he was asked to paint the portrait of a lady who he had previously admired when he was sketching. The lady, Anne Leslie, widow of John Leslie, 11th Earl of Rothes, was 12 years his senior and mother of 3 children. Within a month she became his wife, also bringing with her a personal fortune. They soon visited Italy, armed with letters of introduction supplied by Sir Joshua Reynolds, President of the Royal Academy in London.

After two years of study in Italy they returned to Edinburgh in 1787 where he began to paint portraits of the upper echelons of Scottish Society. He was in constant demand, and at the turn of the century, held a near monopoly of portraiture in Scotland.

In 1799 he moved his studio from 18 George Street to 32 York Place, combining the rear windows to create a large studio. This natural light was controlled by a series of complex shutters. The studio window can still be seen at the rear of the building.

In a letter to London publishers, Cadell and Davis in 1803, Raeburn mentioned that he had recently completed a copy of Nasmyth's portrait of Robert Burns, which was intended as the frontispiece for a new edition of Burns' poems.

On 22nd February 1804 he wrote to Cadell & Davis, *"Gentlemen, Nothing would be more gratifying to me than the approbation you expressed of the Copy I made for you of Robt. Burns. I hope you will be equally pleased with the portrait I now send you by the order of Mr Henry Mackenzie. It is shipped on board the Glasgow Willm Libum Master and I have no doubt you will receive it safe – I am respectfully Gentlemen your most obed srv Henry Raeburn."*

The portrait has never been found. Further mention is made of it in a letter to the British Medical Journal of 4th April 1914.

Around 1790 he painted the portrait known as *The Skating Minister*, but actually titled, *The Reverend Robert Walker skating on Duddingston Loch*. The reverend was the minister of Canongate Kirk which was the church Agnes McLehose, Burns' Clarinda, attended. The Edinburgh Skating Club was the first figure skating club in the world.

Raeburn returned to Edinburgh from Italy in the latter part of Burns' time in Edinburgh and it is unlikely they would have met. However, John Beugo, the engraver, who was a friend of Burns, made engravings from many of Raeburn's paintings in his studio in The Luckenbooths.

Through marriage Raeburn acquired Deanburgh Estate in Stockbridge, later purchasing the neighbouring St Bernard's Estate and amassing a considerable fortune by feuing both estates to build the Stockbridge extension of the New Town. An inventory of his estate when he died showed that he was owed the then large sum of £3526 18s from the rich and famous for their portraits.

Sir Henry Raeburn died intestate at his home at St Bernard's House, Stockbridge, Edinburgh on 8th July 1823. His memorial is in the Church of St John the Evangelist and he was buried in the enclosure at the east end of St John's Church (Scottish Episcopal) at the west end of Princes Street.

Above: Raeburn's enlarged studio window

Below: Sir Henry Raeburn, based on a self-portrait

St James Square
EH1 3SS

During his second stay in Edinburgh, Burns lived for many months in this square as did several of his friends. He also attended a Jacobite dinner in a tavern here.

In the late 16th century, in the Old Town of Edinburgh, the Royal Mile and the warren of closes and lanes that surrounded it were reaching breaking point; overcrowding and very unsanitary conditions resulted in frequent outbreaks of disease.

In order to ease the overcrowding and prevent an exodus of the rich and famous from the city, a competition was held in 1766 to design a 'New Town' north of what is now Princes Street Gardens. The competition was won by the 22-year-old James Craig who designed the present rectangular

Right: Map of St James Square Area 1819

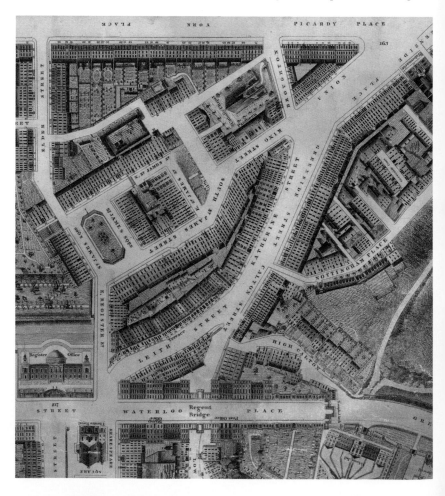

development from St Andrew Square to Charlotte Square and the grid of streets in between.

Work was painfully slow to start and Craig designed a further development, St James Square, which was completed around 1773. At this time only St Andrew Square and parts of the adjoining streets of the main development had been completed and these new tenements allowed professional people, such as teachers and lawyers to escape from the squalor of the High Street. When the New Town was finally finished in 1800, only the wealthy could afford to reside there.

Robert Burns was to live in St James Square on his stay in Edinburgh from 20th October 1787 to 18th February 1788. He lodged with William Cruikshank, Willie Nicol's colleague at Edinburgh High School, Burns referring to this address in letters as, St James Square, No. 2d, Attic Story.

St James Square was a busy area in these years. Robert Ainslie, Alexander Nasmyth, John Beugo, George Thomson and Alexander Cunningham are only a few of the people Burns knew well who either lived or worked in the square.

Burns was staying here when he sustained the injury to his knee which prevented him from visiting Clarinda (Agnes McLehose). It was most likely a dislocated kneecap and Burns blamed it on a careless carriage driver who caused him to fall from the carriage. He was attended by his friend Dr Alexander Wood and was confined to his attic room.

It has also been suggested that Burns may simply have fallen when alighting due to inebriation. All three are possible but it should be noted that Burns did not often drink to excess when in Edinburgh as he was generally working; whether attending an evening soirée where he would be reciting poetry, or at his publisher checking proofs being made ready for printing. He attended French lessons with his friend Beugo at 9 o'clock in the evening, as he was too busy working during the daytime.

Above: Dr Alexander Wood

Below: St James Square c1956

While Burns was stuck in his attic rooms unable to move he wrote the famous Sylvander letters to which Agnes replied as Clarinda. There were some 80 letters in all. In the same attic rooms, Agnes' housemaid, Jenny Clow who had been delivering her mistress's letters and returning for Burns' reply, conceived Burns' son Robert Burns II.

While Burns was trapped by his injury, Agnes would walk from her flat in Potterrow hoping to see Burns at his window – while trying to remain discreet. Given the numbers of people they both knew

who lived or worked around St James Square, as a married woman she risked great scandal if discovered.

One description of his flat was that Burns had *"front and back rooms with bay windows, one looking over St James Square while the other looked over St Andrew Square"*. This would not have been possible from No. 2 as it appears in the Kirkwood map of 1819 and we haven't been able to find any record of a renumbering of the square before that date.

However, another description states that Burns stayed in *"a house on the south west corner of St James Square, topmost or attic window in the gable looking towards the General Post Office in Waterloo Place"*. The attic window in the gable, or end wall, of the building would fit Agnes's account of being able to look for Robert at his window when she passed by.

On 26th December 1787 Burns replied to an invitation to a Jacobite dinner by James Stewart. James Mackay's *Complete Letters* confirms that Stewart was the keeper of Cleland's Gardens, a public house in North St James Street where a dinner was to be held to celebrate the birthday of Prince Charles Edward Stuart, The Young Pretender, on 31st December 1787. In his reply Burns notes *"the honour you do me by your invitation, I most cordially and gratefully accept"*. Burns by then, had recovered enough to walk. Prince Charles Edward Stuart (also known as Bonnie Prince Charlie in retrospective accounts) died barely a month later on 30th January 1788.

Above: Prince Charles Edward Stuart in later life

Robert Burns left St James Square on 18th February 1788 and only 5 days later was reunited with the heavily pregnant Jean Armour in Mauchline, who on 3rd March gave birth to twins, but both died.

By the mid-1900s the St James Square area was deemed by the local council to be unsanitary and unfit for habitation, and by 1960 virtually all of the houses had been demolished to make way for a shopping centre.

Sadly, No. 2 was one of these buildings that were cleared. There is a row of flats backing onto the grounds of West Register House, now a student hostel that still exists; though the roof and upper stories have been substantially altered.

In the corner, in a little garden square, looking partly onto St Andrew Square, are numbers 24 and 25 St James Square, the only surviving parts of the original buildings. While not exactly the same as the building Robert Burns lived in for a short period, they have been restored and are indicative of the style of the late 1700s.

It is sadly ironic that an area that once housed such a very artistic and talented group of people was controversially rebuilt as a "lump of concrete" that forms the St James Centre – one of the most architecturally horrific buildings that has ever been conceived. A critic at the time likened it to Alcatraz; he was being very kind.

Birthday Ode
for the 31st December 1787

Afar the illustrious Exile roams,
Whom kingdoms on this day should hail;
An inmate in the casual shed,
On transient pity's bounty fed,
Haunted by busy memory's bitter tale!
Beasts of the forest have their savage homes,
But He, who should imperial purple wear,
Owns not the lap of earth where rests his
  royal head!
His wretched refuge, dark despair,
While ravening wrongs and woes pursue,
And distant far the faithful few
Who would his sorrows share.

False flatterer, Hope, away!
Nor think to lure us as in days of yore:
We solemnize this sorrowing natal day,
To prove our loyal truth – we can no more,
And owning Heaven's mysterious sway,
Submissive, low adore.

Ye honored, mighty Dead,
Who nobly perished in the glorious cause,
Your King, your Country, and her laws,

From great Dundee, who smiling Victory led,
And fell a Martyr in her arms,
(What breast of northern ice but warms!)
To bold Balmerino's undying name,
Whose soul of fire, lighted at Heaven's high
  flame,
Deserves the proudest wreath departed
  heroes claim:
Nor unrevenged your fate shall lie,
It only lags, the fatal hour,

Your blood shall, with incessant cry,
Awake at last, th' unsparing Power;
As from the cliff, with thundering course,
The snowy ruin smokes along
With doubling speed and gathering force,
Till deep it, crushing, whelms the cottage in
  the vale;
So Vengeance' arm, ensanguin'd, strong,
Shall with resistless might assail,
Usurping Brunswick's pride shall lay,
And Stewart's wrongs and yours, with
  tenfold weight repay.

Perdition, baleful child of night!
Rise and revenge the injured right
Of Stewart's royal race:
Lead on the unmuzzled hounds of hell,
Till all the frighted echoes tell
The blood-notes of the chase!
Full on the quarry point their view,
Full on the base usurping crew,
The tools of faction, and the nation's curse!
Hark how the cry grows on the wind;
They leave the lagging gale behind,
Their savage fury, pitiless, they pour;
With murdering eyes already they devour;
See Brunswick spent, a wretched prey,
His life one poor despairing day,
Where each avenging hour still ushers in a
  worse!
Such havock, howling all abroad,
Their utter ruin bring,
The base apostates to their God,
  Or rebels to their King.

Sylvander and Clarinda

When Burns and Agnes met at Miss Nimmo's tea party on 4th December 1787, in Alison Square, there was a mutual attraction, Agnes immediately inviting him to her house on 6th December but for some reason Burns could not keep this appointment, agreeing to meet her on Saturday 8th.

After wining and dining on 7th December, Burns took a horse-drawn Hackney cab back to the flat in St James Square. For whatever reason – his fault, the coachman's fault, an accident – Burns fell from the coach and seems to have dislocated his kneecap. He must have been helped upstairs because he was living in the top flat, and a friend and neighbour, Alexander Wood, a surgeon, tended to his leg.

Burns had intended leaving Edinburgh in that week, even though he regretted that this would mean he would not see his new acquaintance, Agnes. However, even after resting his leg on a cushion for a few days, he was still confined to the house and had to use crutches to get around. [For lovers of puns: Burns was staying in a flat owned by Cruikshank; in Scots, 'shank'=leg and 'cruik'=crooked!]

Depressed by this confinement which had upset all his plans, Burns began a voluminous, some say somewhat insincere, correspondence with Agnes.

Around 20th December, Agnes suggested that in their many letters, they start referring to each other as 'Sylvander' (Burns) and 'Clarinda' (Agnes). In the 18th century, there was much discussion of proper ways to write letters and the pretention of calling each other names like this was not uncommon. 'Sylvander' means 'man of the woods', the name of a character in a 1786 novel which had been published in Edinburgh; 'Clarinda' meaning beautiful, or bright, was a name used by the Elizabethan poet Edmund Spenser in *The Faerie Queen*.

Above: Dr Alexander Wood after John Kay

Perhaps it was not just pretension on Agnes' part – she may have wished to disguise the identities of these very frequent letter writers from possible gossips. Whatever the reason, Burns liked this conceit and continued to refer to Agnes as Clarinda.

Agnes McLehose has become known worldwide as Clarinda.

On Sunday 31st December Burns managed to leave the flat on crutches to attend a dinner for the 67th birthday of Charles Edward Stuart. Fortunately, it was held in Cleland's Gardens on the corner of St James Square, so he did not have to move far. Besides, Agnes was on holiday in Clackmannan.

It was not until January 4th 1788 that the two letter-writers could meet again. His leg still not mended, Burns travelled by sedan chair to General's Entry where he found Agnes had a headache, but they stayed together from 5pm to 6pm while Agnes listened to Burns' life story.

On the 12th December they met again in the same place, but for their next meeting Agnes asked Burns to come "*by foot*" lest the neighbours hear the arrival of yet another sedan chair. She was very aware of the scandal that would ensue if she, a married woman, became the subject of gossip concerning herself and Burns.

Another meeting on the 18th December was rather tense.

The following day, Burns was ill and Agnes attended a service by the Reverend John Kemp at the Tolbooth church. Biographer James Mackay describes Kemp as a *"sanctimonious lecher"* and he was just the kind of *"Holy Willie"* that Burns could not abide, but his *"fire and brimstone"* sermons shook the deeply religious Agnes.

On their fifth meeting on 23rd January they got very close – perhaps even physically. But Agnes' conscience was getting the better of her.

Burns wrote a song for Clarinda. The following day, Burns wrote in one of his letters to her that he had been drinking with Mr Schekty and that he had *"set the song finely"*. The song was *Clarinda, Mistress of my Soul*.

January 25th 1788, Burns' 29th birthday, found him depressed. This is an important date in his relationship with Agnes' maid Jenny Clow. They forsook Peter Williamson's Penny Post because they were sending so many letters that the cost was no longer insignificant. Also, Agnes was worried that those carrying the letters must have known the identities of the recipients and it could only be a matter of time before the relationship became common knowledge.

So, Jenny was sent to Burns with the letter from Clarinda on the 25th. Approximately nine months later, Jenny was to give birth to Burns' son Robert II.

On Saturday 26th Burns brought his friend Robert Ainslie with him to meet Agnes, and her friend Mary Peacock was also present.

When Burns was told that May Cameron was pregnant in 1787 – Burns had no conscience about having other women while professing love for Agnes; he was unattached after all – it was Ainslie he turned to, to sort things out.

Ainslie was to develop a fondness for Agnes, eventually taking the place of his friend in her company. He became Agnes' lawyer and took on her son Andrew as his pupil.

When Burns next met Agnes, they quarrelled – her devout religious beliefs were getting in the way, and Agnes considered telling William Craig, her cousin and financial benefactor, about her love for Burns.

She mentioned to Burns: *"Mary Peacock fancies you, but knows you fancy me."*

Burns persuaded Agnes to sit for a Miers silhouette, making this the only reliable portrait we have of her. He said to her; *"I want it for a breast pin, to wear next to my heart."* When Burns died, it is said that Jean Armour stitched this breast pin into his shirt and that he was buried with it.

Despite Burns asking her to be chaperoned, she actually went to Miers' studio alone which was a very bold action.

By this time Burns no longer needed crutches and was making preparations to leave Edinburgh. Gossip had reached

Below: Clarinda silhouette after Miers

William Craig and, accompanied by the Reverend Kemp, they rebuked Agnes, warning her of the rumours and reminding her that she was a married woman. At that stage, fortunately, they did not appear to know for certain that the man she had been seeing was Burns.

Burns and Agnes met on Valentine's Day at 8pm. Two days later they discussed Burns' plans to leave Edinburgh and Agnes gave him two shirts as a gift for Jean Armour's son, Robert.

Burns returned to Edinburgh in 1791, after Agnes wrote informing him that Jenny Clow was dying. Hearing that Clarinda was about to go to Jamaica to her husband, the two lovers met for the final time on 6th December.

On the 27th December he sent her *Ae Fond Kiss*, surely the most poignant love song ever written.

Sylvander to Clarinda

When dear Clarinda, matchless fair,
First struck Sylvander's raptur'd view,
He gaz'd, he listened to despair,
Alas! 'twas all he dared to do.

Love, from Clarinda's heavenly eyes,
Transfixed his bosom thro' and thro';
But still in Friendships' guarded guise,
For more the demon fear'd to do.

That heart, already more than lost,
The imp beleaguer'd all perdue;
For frowning Honour kept his post
To meet that frown, he shrunk to do.

His pangs the Bard refused to own,
Tho' half he wish'd Clarinda knew;
But Anguish wrung the unweeting groan
Who blames what frantic Pain must do?

That heart, where motley follies blend,
Was sternly still to Honour true:
To prove Clarinda's fondest friend,
Was what a lover sure might do.

The Muse his ready quill employed,
No nearer bliss he could pursue;
That bliss Clarinda cold deny'd
"Send word by Charles how you do!"

The chill behest disarm'd his muse,
Till passion all impatient grew:
He wrote, and hinted for excuse,
'Twas, 'cause "he'd nothing else to do."

But by those hopes I have above!
And by those faults I dearly rue!
The deed, the boldest mark of love,
For thee that deed I dare to do!

O could the Fates but name the price
Would bless me with your charms and you!
With frantic joy I'd pay it thrice,
If human art and power could do!

Then take, Clarinda, friendship's hand,
(Friendship, at least, I may avow;)
And lay no more your chill command,
I'll write whatever I've to do.

Sylvander.

John Beugo
1759–1841 Engraver

John Beugo was born in Edinburgh and after an apprenticeship he set up in business as an engraver. He is listed in *Williamson's Directory* as staying in Morrison's Close in 1784–85 then having a brief stay in Princes Street before settling into Scales Stair in Blackfriars Wynd from 1788.

In 1867 the eastern side of Blackfriars Wynd, along with the western side of the parallel Todries Wynd, were demolished to create the wider Blackfriars Street, which runs from the High Street to the Cowgate.

He married Elizabeth McDowall, who was also from Edinburgh, and they had one daughter.

He was admitted to The Royal Company of Archers on 26th December 1795.

Beugo first met Burns when Creech employed him to make a copperplate engraving of the Nasmyth portrait for the *Edinburgh Edition*. Like Nasmyth he did not charge for this work.

Burns made additional sittings for the engraving in 1787 and had many copies of it made to give not only to friends but also to hand out when on his Highland and Borders tours, much like a modern-day celebrity with signed photos.

Burns and Beugo became close friends, even attending French classes together in Louis Cauvin's home, most likely in Craig's Close. (see Craig's Close, p.110)

In 1802 Beugo made a line engraving of the drawing by Archibald Skirving. Skirving had never met Burns and his drawing was based on the Nasmyth portrait.

Beugo became the leading Scottish engraver of the time, working on portraits by Raeburn and also designing bank notes. He was secretary of the first exhibition of paintings held in Sir Henry Raeburn's rooms in York Place.

John Beugo died in 1841 and is buried in Greyfriars Kirkyard.

Below: John Beugo

William Cruikshank

1746–95 Teacher

William Cruikshank was born in Duns and was trained as a teacher by his uncle, also named William, a schoolmaster at Duns.

In 1770 William Cruikshank was appointed Rector of the High School in the Canongate before becoming Latin Master of the High School in 1772 where he worked alongside Willie Nicol.

Through his friendship with Nicol, William Cruikshank rented out accommodation to Burns on his return to Edinburgh in the autumn of 1787 until Burns left Edinburgh in February 1788.

William Cruikshank is buried in an unmarked grave, to the east of the obelisk to the political martyrs, in Old Calton Burial Ground.

On Cruikshank's death Burns wrote:

Above: William Cruickshank

Epitaph for Mr W Cruikshank

Honest Will to heaven is gane,
An' mony shall lament him,
His faults they all in Latin lay,
In English nane e'er kent them.

Jean Cruikshank

c1775–1835 Daughter of William Cruikshank

Cruikshank's daughter Jean, or Jeany as she was known, often played piano or harpsichord accompaniment for Burns when he was working on his songs; even though she was only 12 years old.

She was very talented and Burns complimented her by writing *To Miss Cruikshank* and *A Rosebud by My Early Walk* for her.

She became the wife of James Henderson, a writer (lawyer) in Jedburgh, and when she died in 1835, aged around 60, she was buried in Jedburgh Abbey.

A Rosebud by My Early Walk

A Rosebud by my early walk,
Adown a corn-enclosed bawk,
Sae gently bent its thorny stalk
All on a dewy morning.
Ere twice the shades o' dawn are fled,
In a' its crimson glory spread,
And drooping rich the dewy head,
It scents the early morning.

Within the bush her covert nest
A little linnet fondly prest,
The dew sat chilly on her breast
Sae early in the morning.
She soon shall see her tender brood
The pride, the pleasure o' the wood,
Amang the fresh green leaves bedew'd,
Awauk the early morning.

So thou, dear bird, young Jeany fair,
On trembling string or vocal air,
Shalt sweetly pay the tender care
That tents thy early morning.
So thou, sweet Rosebud, young and gay,
Shalt beauteous blaze upon the day,
And bless the Parent's evening ray
That watch'd thy early morning.

The Jacobite Rebellions and Tartan

James VII of Scotland and II of England was deposed in 1688 and the throne was claimed by his daughter Mary II and her husband William of Orange. The Jacobite Rebellions were a series of uprisings, the aim of which was to restore the House of Stuart to the throne after the Stuarts were deposed by the English Parliament in 1688. The Act of Union (Union with England Act) was passed in 1707 by the Parliament of Scotland. The two major rebellions were in 1715 and 1745.

The 1715 Jacobite Rebellion was precipitated by the refusal of the supporters of James VII of Scotland and II of England to swear the anti-Catholic oath. But this attempt to restore the Stuarts represented by the son of James VII of Scotland and II of England, James Francis Edward Stuart (The Old Pretender) failed.

A second Jacobite Rebellion in 1745 failed to restore James Francis Edward Stuart's son, Charles Edward Stuart (The Young Pretender) to the throne.

After the failure of the '45 Rebellion the government brought in laws designed to *"bring peace to the Highlands"*. One of these was The Act of Proscription incorporating The Dress Act (August 1746) which banned the wearing of tartan (or plaid – pronounced 'plaad' – as it was known). All swords had to be surrendered to the government and permission was required to carry any weapon. The government put extra troops into the Highlands to enforce this 'peace', often with excessive force and brutality.

It was not until 1782 that the Dress Act was repealed. As a lowlander Robert Burns would not have had a reason to wear tartan.

Charles Edward Stuart, popularly known as Bonnie Prince Charlie, died on 30th January 1788. As we know, Burns attended a Jacobite dinner in St James Square, Edinburgh on 31st December 1787 to celebrate the 68th birthday of the Prince. Burns was a supporter of the Jacobite cause but was very well aware of the political situation and the potential repercussions for falling foul of the British Government – for which he would shortly be working as an excise officer.

Below: A young 'Bonnie Prince Charlie'

In 1822 George IV visited Edinburgh; this was the first visit to Scotland by a reigning monarch since 1650, a period of 172 years. It was George IV's visit and rather remarkable tartan attire which then introduced the fashion of tartan as a national dress.

A series of pageants was organised by Sir Walter Scott and, as the King had agreed to wear a kilt, Scott advised that apart from those in uniform, "*no gentleman would be allowed to appear in anything but the ancient highland costume*". Edinburgh tailors struggled to find suitable attire, and much of the tartan was borrowed from the Highland Regiments who, ironically, had been authorised to wear it during the ban in an effort to make them appear more 'Scottish', at a time when Scots themselves were forbidden to wear tartan.

George IV's outfit for the final pageant, a Highland Ball, created in a bright red tartan, now known as Royal Stewart, cost the equivalent today of £110,000.

Such a Parcel Of Rogues In A Nation

Fareweel to a' our Scottish fame,
Fareweel our ancient glory,
Fareweel ev'n to the Scottish name,
Sae fam'd in martial story.
Now Sark rins o'er the Solway sands,
And Tweed rins to the ocean,
To mark where England's province stands –
Such a parcel of rogues in a nation!

What force or guile could not subdue,
Thro' many warlike ages,
Is wrought now by a coward few
For hireling traitor's wages.
The English steel we could disdain;
Secure in valour's station;
But English gold has been our bane –
Such a parcel of rogues in a nation!

O would, or I had seen the day
That treason thus could sell us,
My auld gray head had lien in clay,
Wi' Bruce and loyal Wallace!
But pith and power, till my last hour,
I'll mak' this declaration;
We're bought and sold for English gold –
Such a parcel of rogues in a nation!

Theatre Royal
Shakespeare Square, near EH2 2EQ

Robert Fergusson, Robert Burns and Sir Walter Scott, all in their time, regularly attended this theatre.

From the front of Register House look directly across Princes Street to the left of North Bridge. The large sandstone building on the corner (now called Waverley Gate – a façade retention concept) is the former General Post Office building which now occupies the site of Shakespeare's Square and the former Theatre Royal.

Nothing whatsoever is left of what was for almost 90 years the premier theatrical venue in Scotland. Regarded as the 'national theatre', it was host to some of the biggest names in the acting profession in the 18th and 19th centuries and the scene of many great productions, written by the country's greatest writers.

Below: Theatre Royal Edinburgh
c1830

The original design of founder David Ross's theatre of 1769 is a rather stark neo-classical façade. Its interior comprised of a curved auditorium with pit, a complete box tier with side boxes, an upper gallery, centre gallery, and orchestra pit. The building was 57-feet-wide by 90-feet-high and 108 feet in length, with an audience capacity of approximately 600. The frontage was remodelled in 1816 and again more extensively in 1828. The building remained in that style until it was demolished in 1859.

It would take a book many times the size of this to do justice to the story of the Theatre Royal; this section focuses only on the era of Robert Burns and shortly thereafter.

There can be little doubt that, if he had lived, it would have been a natural progression for Robert Burns to have written for theatre. He was an enthusiastic and regular theatre-goer, not only at the Edinburgh Theatre Royal but also at the Theatre Royal in Dumfries.

"Strange to recal [sic] the circumstances of the theatre at its opening. No Princes Street then for the belles and beaux—no New Town whatever—only one or two houses building at wide intervals. The North Bridge unfinished and broken down; ladies and gentlemen obliged to come to these mimic scenes through Leith Wynd and other and still narrower alleys. Owing partly to these causes, partly to want, of attraction in the company, Mr Ross had two unsuccessful seasons."

– From the volume *Sketch of the History Of The Edinburgh Theatre Royal Prepared for this Evening of its Final Closing*, May 25, 1859.

Above: Site Map of Theatre Royal Edinburgh 1794

Left: Theatre Royal Facade 1769

Front of THEATRE *towards* Princes Street

- - - - - - - - - - *Extends 54 Feet* - - - - - - - - -

90

David Ross
1728–90 Theatre owner and actor

Above: David Ross

David Ross was born in London in 1728, the son of Alexander Ross, a Writer to the Signet in Edinburgh, who had moved to London in 1722 as a Solicitor of Appeals. David had a difficult relationship with his father who disowned him when he was 13, eventually disinheriting him.

He was engaged by renowned theatre owner and actor David Garrick in 1751, and made his first Drury Lane appearance in *The Conscious Lovers* – this play would be the inaugural performance at what would become Ross's Theatre Royal, Edinburgh. While he played a wide variety of roles, his *pièce de résistance* was said to be as Hamlet.

In 1767 Ross moved to Edinburgh and after a bitter legal battle gained a Royal Patent for the Canongate Theatre. The strength of opposition to the establishment of the theatre from the Church of Scotland can be judged by one churchgoer's exhortation to his Kirk Session to: *"break down the theatres and banish those idle dogs the actors to the mines, there to work under severe discipline and harsh punishment"*.

However, Ross managed to raise half the building costs of £5,000 for a new theatre with a subscription, and laid the foundation stone in Shakespeare's Square in March 1768. Ross's Theatre Royal opened on the 9th of December 1769, the performance being preceded with an address written by his good friend James Boswell.

It was a desperately disappointing first season for Ross. On the 3rd August, just four months prior to the opening night, the partly erected North Bridge which had been opened to pedestrians, collapsed killing 5 workers. The bridge, which had already cost more than double the original estimate, did not open fully until 1772.

The complete closure of the North Bridge meant that, with little or no construction yet started on the New Town, the Theatre Royal became isolated. It would be several years before audiences were sufficient in numbers to regularly attract the productions and stars to be found on the London stage.

After letting out the theatre to various managers over the next 12 years, Ross sold the theatre to John Jackson.

In his later years, complications with a badly broken leg led to ill health, which was exacerbated by his once indulgent lifestyle, and led to serious financial problems.

He was supported financially by friends and he died in London in 1790 at the age of 62. The chief mourner at his funeral in St James's Piccadilly, was his faithful friend James Boswell.

It is widely accepted that Ross's dream and fight to establish a theatre in Edinburgh helped lay the foundations of a Scottish national theatre.

John Home
1722–1808 Playright

John Home (pronounced 'Hume'), was born in 1722 in Leith and was for a time a Church of Scotland minister and a playwright, at the time two completely opposing occupations.

His first play was written in 1749, a tragedy based on a King of Sparta titled *Agis*. His second play, and hugely successful, was another tragedy set in Viking-era Scotland called *Douglas*.

Initially rejected by London theatre impresario David Garrick as *"totally unfit for the stage"*, it opened at the Canongate Theatre in Edinburgh on the 14th December 1756 to great critical acclaim.

After seeing the play, Robert Burns was moved to write of *"the horrors I felt for Lady Randolph's distresses"*.

Douglas caused a great religious furore in Edinburgh leaving Home's position as a minister untenable, forcing him to resign in June 1757.

The play was popular for almost a hundred years, and starred a host of the most famous actors of the 18th and 19th centuries. These included the Kemble acting dynasty and the legendary Sarah Siddons who played the part of Lady Randolph many times.

Henry Erskine Johnston's portrayal of Norval was said by Home to be the greatest performance of the part that he had ever seen.

Douglas transferred well and was very popular in American theatre, but by the mid-19th century was looked upon as being old-fashioned, and is now rarely performed.

Home had another three successful plays staged: *The Fatal Discovery* (1769), *Alonzo* (1773), and *Alfred* (1778).

Walter Scott, then in his late 20s, was a regular visitor to Home's house.

David Home died at his villa near Merchiston, Edinburgh in 1808.

Above: John Home

Below, left: Woods, Siddons and Sutherland by John Kay

Below: Sarah Siddons as Lady Randolph

William Woods
1749–1802 Actor

The details of William Woods early years are few, but it is thought that he first worked in the printing trade.

He first appeared on the London stage at the Haymarket Theatre in 1771 before travelling to Edinburgh, where he was to spend the next 31 years of his life.

Woods was described as *"a capable actor … without a blemish to his character and of gentlemanly manners and address"*.

He was a close friend of the poet Robert Fergusson and would be on hand to take him to his seat before the doors opened to the public. Fergusson was reported to have *"applauded in a most peculiar manner, bringing his fist down like a hammer on the top of the rail in front of the dress circle"*.

Woods was a member of Lodge Canongate Kilwinning No. 2 and it is likely that Burns and Woods met here, but, as a regular theatre-goer Burns would also have met Woods at the Theatre Royal. They became very good friends and Burns wrote a prologue, which referenced the actress Sarah Siddons, for Woods' benefit night on the 16th April 1787.

Woods acted in countless roles at the Theatre Royal, often playing alongside his actress wife Ann. His first role at the Theatre Royal was as Glenalvon, in John Home's *Douglas*, on the 27th of January 1772. He played the Ghost to Henry Erskine Johnston's first performance as Hamlet on the 11th June 1794.

By 1800, Woods, although still very popular with the theatre-going public, was being passed over for roles by younger actors. His health was failing and he decided to retire gracefully. At his farewell benefit on the 19th April 1802, it was reported that *"the plaudits of the audience when he finally retired were quite unprecedented"*.

William Woods died on 14th December 1802, aged 53, from apoplexy at his home in 14 Leith Terrace. He is buried in the Old Calton Burial Ground, where, around 1862, his headstone was replaced by Victorian theatre enthusiasts, the new headstone engraved with suitable Shakespearian quotes.

Above: William Woods as Glenalvon in Home's *Douglas*, in 1798

Right, inset: Playbill for *Rob Roy*, performed at Theatre Royal, Edinburgh, 11th March 1829

Prologue spoken by Mr Woods

When by a generous Public's kind acclaim,
That dearest meed is granted-honest fame;
When here your favour is the actor's lot,
Nor even the man in private life forgot;
What breast so dead to heav'nly Virtue's glow,
But heaves impassion'd with the grateful throe.

Poor is the task to please a barb'rous throng,
It needs no Siddons' powers in Southern's song;
But here an ancient nation fam'd afar,
For genius, learning high, as great in war –
Hail, Caledonia, name for ever dear!
Before whose sons I'm honour'd to appear!

Where every science – every nobler art –
That can inform the mind, or mend the heart,
Is known; as grateful nations oft have found
Far as the rude barbarian marks the bound.
Philosophy, no idle pedant dream,
Here holds her search by heaven-taught Reason's beam;
Here History paints, with elegance and force,
The tide of Empire's fluctuating course;
Here Douglas forms wild Shakespeare into plan,

And Harley rouses all the god in man.
When well-form'd taste, and sparkling wit unite,
With manly lore, or female beauty bright,
(Beauty, where faultless symmetry and grace,
Can only charm us in the second place,)
Witness my heart, how oft with panting fear,
As on this night, I've met these judges here!
But still the hope Experience taught to live,
Equal to judge – you're candid to forgive.
No hundred-headed Riot here we meet,
With decency and law beneath his feet;
Nor Insolence assumes fair Freedom's name;
Like Caledonians, you applaud or blame.

O thou, dread Power! Whose empire-giving hand
Has oft been stretch'd to shield the honour'd land!
Strong may she glow with all her ancient fire;
May every son be worthy of his sire;
Firm may she rise with generous disdain
At Tyranny's, or direr Pleasure's chain;
Still self-dependent in her native shore,
Bold may she brave grim Danger's loudest roar,
Till Fate the curtain drop on worlds to be no more.

Walter Scott Author

From a young age Walter Scott began a long association with the Edinburgh Theatre Royal, maintaining close friendships with many of the principal actors and managers involved, especially John Philip Kemble and Sarah Siddons. Indeed most of the stage adaptations of his novels were premiered at the theatre.

Scott also helped to produce plays written by other authors and playwrights which were first staged in Edinburgh before touring other Scottish theatres.

Scott's first connection with the Edinburgh Theatre Royal was in a drama of a different sort in 1794 when he was 23 years old. A violent altercation ensued when a group of Irish students refused to stand during the playing of *God Save The King* at the end of a performance. During the melée cudgels and staves were in evidence with *"broken heads and bones"* on both sides.

Scott was later bound over by the magistrates to keep the peace, but claimed victory, as the opposing side failed to appear for a re-match the following day.

(The only meeting between Walter Scott and Robert Burns took place in Sciennes Hill House, the home of Professor Adam Ferguson in 1787, when Scott was 15 years old. (see p.160))

Below: Walter Scott in his 20s

Old Calton Burial Ground

27 Waterloo Place, EH1 3BQ

1 27 Waterloo Place

2 14 Calton Hill

3 Dugald Stewart Monument

4 Burns' Monument

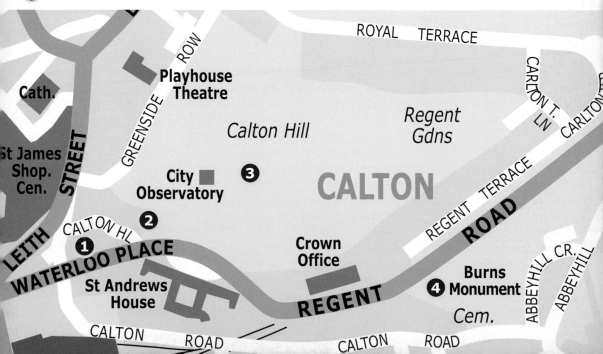

Adjacent to the Burns Monument is a pathway that exits on Calton Road below. This is a steep and uneven path and is not suitable for wheelchair users or those without full mobility. From Calton Road, pedestrians may use Campbell's Close which exits on Canongate.

The burial place of many of Burns' friends and contemporaries; it is also the location of the first statue to Abraham Lincoln outside America.

The importance of Old Calton Burial Ground in the history of Edinburgh is reflected in its status as a New Town Conservation Area as well as an Edinburgh World Heritage Site.

At the time of Burns' stay in Edinburgh this was one of the main burial places in the city and many with strong connections to him found their last resting places here.

In the late 1500s a small hospital was created at the foot of the hill following an outbreak of leprosy. Those infected had to stay for 40 days and nights before being declared free of the disease.

Below: Old Calton Burial Ground

The dead were buried in pits nearby and gallows were erected on Calton Hill to deal with escapees. The gallows were also used to dispatch condemned witches.

Originally a rocky ridge, Calton Hill was used for grazing and quarrying for several centuries prior to the urban expansion of Edinburgh in the 1760s.

Old Calton Burial Ground was the first major development of the hill when, in 1718, the Society of Incorporated Trades of Calton received permission to use the land as a burial ground. The area at this time was outwith the bounds of the city, but the society was based in the Parish of Leith where land was unsuitable and Old Calton provided a convenient burial ground.

Throughout the 1700s, as Greyfriars Churchyard in the Old Town became overcrowded, and as the New Town was developing, the Old Calton Burial Ground expanded into adjoining land. Then, when Regent Road was built in 1816–19, the new road cut through, dividing the burial ground in two. Bodies, soil and headstones, were taken on carts covered with white sheets to be relocated in a cemetery at the bottom of Calton Road. The small section of Old Calton Burial Ground, to the north of Regent Road, can be accessed via an entrance on Calton Hill.

In 1790 regulations were introduced covering payment of lair fees. Those in the centre of the graveyard were cheaper than those around the walls. Only those against the wall were able to enclose the burial area. The fees were also set for a gravedigger to watch over the lair for several days after an internment in an effort to protect the bodies from theft by grave robbers.

Below: Old Calton Burial Ground view to Calton Hill

The burial ground closed in 1869, with management passing from the Incorporated Trades to the Town Council of Edinburgh in 1888.

Some of Burns' friends lie here in unmarked graves:

- William Cruikshank (1746–95): unmarked grave to the east of the obelisk
- Willie Nicol (1747–97): unmarked grave to the east of the obelisk. It was reported that in 1796 he purchased 5 lairs close to the Hume Memorial
- Peter Williamson ('Indian Peter') (1730–99): unmarked grave to the north-east of the obelisk
- John Playfair (1748–1819): scientist, astrologer, mathematician, philosopher and geologist. The lair is made up of 3 walls with a small step and is close by Hume's tomb and adjacent to the grave of Julius Yelin. Although his grave is unmarked, the monument to John Playfair on Calton Hill overlooks his final resting place.

On the other side of the burial ground, behind the Lincoln Statue, lying sadly neglected, is the Robert Burn Mausoleum. It was Burn the architect who created the gravestone at Fergusson's grave in the Kirk of the Canongate at the request of Robert Burns. He was a highly respected and

Left: Robert Burn (architect) Mausoleum

Below: The Scottish Parliament Cairn, and its plaque.

much sought after architect, designing Nelson's Monument on Calton Hill.

As well as many other Edinburgh buildings he was also commissioned to design the new front portico to the Assembly Rooms in George Street as it was felt that the original, and rather plain facade, was not quite grand enough.

A more recent addition to Calton Hill is the Scottish Parliament Cairn. A cairn is a man-made stack of stones. (The word 'cairn' is from Scottish Gaelic: *càrn*). It commemorates the vigil for the Scottish Parliament. The brazier on the top of the cairn was kept burning from 1992 (the evening of the fourth consecutive Conservative general election victory) until 11th September 1997 – the day that Scotland voted for devolution and the restoration of a Scottish Parliament. Built into the cairn are the number of stones gathered from various places – including one from the Mauchline home of Robert Burns and Jean Armour.

Old Calton Burial Ground
27 Waterloo Place
Edinburgh
EH1 3BQ
0131 664 4314
www.edinburgh.gov.uk

Scottish American Memorial

Above: Scottish American Memorial

When, as a teenager in the mid-1820s, Abraham Lincoln stumbled across a collection of Robert Burns' poems, this was to be the beginning of a lifetime's appreciation of his works.

Lincoln memorised many of the poems; *Tam O'Shanter, Holy Willie's Prayer* and *The Cotter's Saturday Night* being among his favourites. In 1859 he attended the Springfield Centenary celebration of Burns' birthday, giving a formal toast to his memory. In 1865, when Lincoln was asked by one of his Scottish-born aides to give recognition of Burns' genius, a note from Lincoln was read at the Burns celebrations:

"I cannot frame a toast to Burns. I can say nothing worthy of his generous heart and transcendent genius. Thinking of what he said, I cannot say anything worth saying."

When James Wilson, editor of Chicago's first literary magazine, wrote to Lincoln and told him that he had been to Prestwick and had spent the whole day speaking with Isabella Burns Begg, Robert's sister, who was then 80 years old, Lincoln expressed his great admiration for his trip to Ayr and Scotland, stating that he hoped to be able to make the same trip himself.

Visitors to the Lincoln family home in Springfield, Massachusetts, may very well have been entertained by Abraham Lincoln reading the work of Burns or Shakespeare to his guests. Following the refurbishment of Lincoln's home in 1988, one of the first objects that visitors see on entering is a bust of Robert Burns.

Many of Lincoln's aides and acquaintances were either born in Scotland or were Scots-American, as were many of the soldiers who fought on the side of the

Union in the American Civil War, soldiers whose families had been emigrating to America since the days of the failed Jacobite rebellions and the Highland Clearances of the early 1800s. However, it comes as a pleasant surprise to find this memorial, *In Memory of Scottish-American Soldiers*, nestling in Old Calton Burial Ground.

It is the first statue to an American President outside the United States; it is also the only memorial to the American Civil War outside the United States.

In the 1860 census, the slave population of the United States was given as 4 million. The American Civil War started in 1861 when Southern slave-holding states, fearing that the institution of slavery was under threat in a nation governed by Northern states, seceded from the US after the election of Abraham Lincoln.

After 4 years of warfare in which an estimated 750,000 soldiers died, the conflict ended in 1865 with the surrender of Southern, or Confederate forces. Slavery was officially abolished by Constitutional Amendment in the same year.

Below: Detail of the Scottish American Memorial

Political Martyrs' Monument

The Political Martyrs' Monument, designed by Thomas Hamilton and erected in 1844, is visible from many parts of Edinburgh. It was dedicated to the memory of Thomas Muir of Huntershill, near Glasgow, as well as Thomas Fyshe Palmer, William Skirving, Maurice Margarot and Joseph Gerrald, who were the leading figures in The Friends of the People, a suffrage movement whose crime in the eyes of the judges was to fight for voting rights for all and not just landowners.

They were arrested on 4th August 1793 and brought to trial, charged with sedition, writing and publishing pamphlets on parliamentary reform. On 30th August 1793 they were banished to Botany Bay in Australia for a period of 14 years.

Once in Australia the men settled into their new lives and all went on to become respected and prosperous citizens.

The Scottish Reform Act of 1832 changed voting rights, bringing about the aims of Muir and the others, and in 1838 all five were pardoned but were not given their passage home.

Palmer, Skirving, Margarot and Gerrald all died in Australia.

At a time when many ports were being blockaded by British warships, Muir staged an escape from Australia in February 1796, a journey that was to take him to Monterey in California, Mexico City and Havana. In Cuba he was jailed for 3 months for trying to escape and was suspected of being a spy. On transportation to Spain, the ship was involved in a battle with the British near Cadiz and Muir was seriously injured; his cheekbone was smashed and he suffered serious injuries to both eyes. As he was smuggled ashore with the injured, the captain announced that Muir had died in the battle, indeed so severe were his injuries that he was not expected to survive. Under pressure from the French Government, the Spanish Government relented and Muir made his way to France, arriving in Bordeaux in November 1797, and finally Paris, on 4th February 1798 where he was hailed a hero of the French Republic and a Martyr of Liberty.

Robert Burns was very well aware of the trial of Muir and the consequences of being labelled a radical and nationalist, warnings that Burns heeded in public at least, publishing his more radical and inflammatory work anonymously.

Thomas Muir was known as the Father of Scottish Democracy. In March 2011, Scotland's First Minister said of Muir '... *his memory should cast a beam across the work of every civil servant in the Scottish Government and every minister – because the monument to Muir and his revolutionaries spikes out of Calton graveyard like a shaft of stony light ...*"

Opposite page: (above (detail) and below) The Political Martyrs' Monument

Thomas Muir died suddenly in Chantilly, France on 26th January 1799.

To Messrs Muir, Palmer, Skirving and Margarot

Friends of the Slighted people – ye whose wrongs
From wounded FREEDOM many a tear shall draw
As once she mourn'd when mocked by venal tongues
Her SYDNEY fell beneath the form of law.

O had this bosom known poetic fire
Your names, your deeds, should grace my votive songs
For Virtue taught the bard's far-sounding lyre
To lift the PATRIOT from the servile throng.

High o'er the wrecks of time his fame shall live
While proud Oppression wastes her idle rage.
IIis name on history's column shall revive
And wake the genius of a distant age.

Below: Thomas Muir

It shines – the dawn of that long promised day
For eager Fancy bursts the midnight gloom
The patriot's praise, the grateful nations pay
And tears the trophy from the oppressor's tomb.

Yet what the praise far distant times shall sing
To that calm solace Virtue now bestows.
Round the dire bark She waves her guardian wing;
She guides her exiles o'er the trackless snows:
With Joy's gay flowers She decks the sultry wild
And sheds the beam of Hope where Nature never smil'd.

David Hume
1711–76 Philosopher

David Hume was renowned across Europe as a philosopher and was a critical figure in the Scottish Enlightenment, regarded as the most important philosopher ever to write in English.

He was born David Home, in a tenement on the north side of the Lawnmarket in Edinburgh, on 7th May 1711. His father died when he was 2 years old and he spent most of his childhood on the small family estate near Berwick. He attended Edinburgh University when he was 12 years old.

After working in Bristol as a merchant's clerk for some time, he travelled to Anjou in France in 1734. It was also at this time that he changed his name to Hume so that the English could easily pronounce the Scottish name of Home in the Scottish manner.

He spent 4 years in France and completed his *Treatise of Human Nature* at the age of 26. Hume wrote many books on a wide variety of subjects, and was a major influence on many of Europe's leading writers and thinkers.

He obtained a position of the Librarian for the Faculty of Advocates, a job that suited his project, *The History of England,* as it gave him access to a vast amount of information. The book was published in 6 volumes and took 15 years to complete, becoming a bestseller and brought him recognition as a historian.

His 1754 order for books for the Advocates Library brought charges of heresy against him in 1756 as the books were regarded as *"indecent and unworthy of a place in a learned library"*. He was finally acquitted, his lawyers apparently successfully arguing that, as an atheist, he was outside the church's jurisdiction.

Above: David Hume

Hume regarded it as a personal insult that the library cancelled the order for the books, but as he needed the resources of the library for his writing, he stayed in the post but turned over his salary to Thomas Blacklock, known as the Blind Poet, whom he had previously befriended and sponsored.

It was Thomas Blacklock who urged Robert Burns to come to Edinburgh where another, larger edition of his book, *Poems Chiefly in the Scottish Dialect* could be published.

When he had completed his research, Hume resigned the post, making it available for Adam Ferguson.

His refusal to acknowledge the existence of God infuriated many members of the Society of Tradesmen of Calton who managed the burial ground.

Six months before his death Hume purchased a lair in Old Calton Burial Ground for £4. David Hume died on Sunday 25th August 1776 at home, at the south-west corner of St Andrew Square. A hostile crowd gathered at his funeral forcing friends and relations of Hume to stand guard over his grave for 8 days afterwards. As well as protecting the grave from desecration from the angry crowd, they also protected the grave from body snatchers who would have removed the body to sell to medical students.

Two years later his nephew petitioned for a further portion of ground to erect the monument, designed by Robert Adam in 1777, which today stands in the south-west corner.

Hume never married. Legend has it that shortly after his death his friends renamed the street on which he lived, and it remains to this day, St David Street. He would have seen the joke.

Left: David Hume Mausoleum

David Allan
1744–96 Artist

Allan was born in Alloa and studied at Foulis Academy. In common with many Scottish painters of the time, he went to Rome from 1768–77 to continue his studies, working under Gavin Hamilton and becoming famous in Rome for his caricatures.

He attempted to establish himself in London as a portrait painter, but struggled to find commissions. Allan then returning to Edinburgh in 1779, later succeeded Alexander Runciman as Master of the Trustees Academy, which was established in Edinburgh for the study of drawing.

He ran a school from Dickson's Close which now forms part of the Radisson Blu Hotel in the Cowgate.

Just before he died he was working on illustrations for Burns' *Scottish Songs,* a work which he never completed. He did, however, paint Burns from the Nasmyth original as a character in *The Cotter's Saturday Night*, painting a young Burns into one of the scenes.

George Thomson made a present of the painting to Robert Burns in 1795, much to the delight of the bard who thought it a great likeness.

After Burns' death, Gilbert Burns, on behalf of Jean Armour, gifted the painting to Mrs Dunlop of Dunlop, with whom Burns had corresponded more than any other person.

Above: David Allan

David Allan died in Edinburgh on 6th August 1796, aged 52, and is buried in Old Calton Burial Ground.

A headstone was erected over the grave in 1874 by the Royal Scottish Academy.

Right: The Cotter's Saturday Night. An engraving from the original drawing by David Allan.

14 Calton Hill
EH1 3BJ

In her later years Burns' Clarinda (Agnes McLehose), lived here,

In 1810 Agnes moved from Potterrow to live at Calton Hill. Her first home No. 3, a tenement flat on the west side of the street near the bottom of the hill, was not in good condition and has long since been demolished. After only a short period of time Agnes moved across the road to No. 14.

The existing No. 14 is **NOT** the same house that Agnes lived in.

Kirkwood maps from 1819 and early Ordnance Survey maps show 8 houses in the row. However, from around 1920 buildings were taken down and by the end of the Second World War, four of the houses from the lower end of the row had gone, one of which would have been the original No. 14. The section towards the bottom of the hill has been completely redesigned and rebuilt.

Once settled in Calton Hill, Agnes became even more involved in Edinburgh society. She was a charming hostess and, with of her knowledge of the arts and bright conversation, was a welcome guest at many evening soirées. For 40 years she held a New Year's Day celebration at her house here in Calton Hill, her invitations being eagerly anticipated.

Agnes liked to walk. After a visit to Calton Hill on 6th December 1831, she wrote in her journal: *"Parted with Burns, in the year 1791, never more to meet in this world. Oh, may we meet in Heaven!"*

Agnes died in her house on Calton Hill, on 22nd October 1841 aged 82.

Above: Calton Hill area 1794

Left: Calton Hill in Burns' time

Below: Calton Hill in the present day

Agnes 'Nancy' McLehose – Clarinda Close friend

1758–1841

Agnes 'Nancy' McLehose was born in Glasgow on the 26th April 1758, the third of 4 daughters of Andrew Craig, a Glasgow surgeon, and Christian McLaurin. 2 of the daughters died young and another, Margaret, died in childbirth in 1771.

In 1767, when Agnes was only 9 years old, her mother also died.

When she was 15, Agnes attended a boarding school in Edinburgh, which involved frequent trips by coach.

She was by all accounts very attractive, petite and blonde, attracting the attention of James McLehose, a Glasgow lawyer who, one day, booked all the seats on the Glasgow to Edinburgh stagecoach so that he could be alone with her for the entire 10-hour journey. Six months later she returned to Glasgow and married James, who was around 5 years her elder, on 1st July 1776 in St Andrews in the Square, Glasgow, near her family home in the Saltmarket. She was now 18 years old.

Below: Agnes McLehose after Miers Silhouette

Agnes and James had 4 children in 5 years. William, their firstborn, died very young. Andrew, the strongest child, was born in June 1778, and a second William in April 1780.

It was not a happy marriage, James was a violent drunkard, *"Our disagreements rose to such a height, and my husband's treatment of me was so harsh, that it was thought advisable by my friends a separation should take place, which accordingly followed in December 1780."*

They separated in December 1780, when Agnes was expecting their fourth child, James, who was born in April 1781.

Homeless and alone, Agnes returned to her father's house in Saltmarket, Glasgow, while her estranged husband obtained custody of both boys, a right under Scottish law he robustly enforced. Shortly after the birth of James, he also took custody of the infant, immediately sending all of the children to his relatives.

Agnes stayed with her father and when he died on 13th May 1782, Agnes inherited *"the second storey of a tenement on the east side of Trongate, household effects and the sum of £50.00"*. This inheritance allowed Agnes to move back to Edinburgh, where she rented a small flat on the first floor of a tenement in a court at the back of General's Entry.

When James found that she had returned to Edinburgh he wrote asking to see her, perhaps the sudden interest was more about her inheritance, but it was a request which she firmly rejected. He responded in a letter from London, by telling her to go to Glasgow and take her children back as *"none of my friends will have anything to do with them"*.

With three infants to support, she managed to obtain small annuities of £10 from The Society of Writers and £8 from Society of Surgeons. This was just enough, if she was careful, to live on.

James McLehose spent some time in London in 1782, where he was thrown into a debtor's prison. His family paid for his release, on condition that he emigrated forthwith and he sailed for Jamaica in November 1784.

James prospered in Jamaica, to the extent that the annuities from the Writers and Surgeon's Societies stopped as he could now support his family; but he made no contact, nor replied to letters. Lord William Craig, Agnes' cousin, then stepped in to provide for her and her family. He looked after her finances and left her an annuity when he died in 1813.

In 1792, James, on hearing that their youngest child had died, sent Agnes £50 and invited Agnes to Jamaica to attempt reconciliation, whereupon, and despite having had no contact with him for three years, she accepted.

It may seem an unlikely course of action for Agnes to take, but gossip about her relationship with Burns may have led Lord William Craig to encourage her to go to Jamaica and escape a possible scandal. By a coincidence, which would seem contrived in fiction, in January 1791, Agnes sailed to Jamaica on the *Roselle*, the very vessel on which Burns had been planning his journey.

James had no intention of reconciliation and did not even meet Agnes on her arrival in Kingston. She was to find that he had taken a native mistress with whom he had a daughter, Ann Lavinia McLehose. The climate made Agnes ill and she returned to Scotland at the first opportunity, never to see her husband again.

Above: Agnes McLehose c1807

James was for many years Chief Clerk to the Court and had a large income – none of which, despite a successful court suit ordering him to pay her £100, was seen by Agnes until his death in 1812 when she received several hundred pounds from James' bank account in London. Now Agnes could live as befitting her position.

Her son, Andrew died in 1839, predeceased by his wife and 2 children. The surviving grandson, William, inherited her estate, including her letters.

Agnes McLehose died on 22nd October 1841, in her 83rd year. She is buried in Canongate Kirkyard.

To a Lady*
with a present of a pair of
drinking glasses

Fair Empress of the Poet's soul,
And Queen of Poetesses;
Clarinda, take this little boon,
This humble pair of Glasses:

And fill them up with generous juice,
As generous as your mind;
And pledge me in the generous toast,
"The whole of human kind!"

"To those who love us!" second fill;
But not to those whom we love;
Lest we love those who love not us
A third – "To thee and me, Love!"

Long may we live! Long may we love!
And long may we be happy!!!
And may we never want a Glass,
Well charg'd with generous Nappy!!!!

* Mrs Agnes McLehose

Professor Dugald Stewart
1753–1828 Philosopher
Calton Hill

Dugald Stewart was born in Edinburgh on 22nd November 1753.

In 1771 he studied at Glasgow University, attending Thomas Reid's classes where he developed his theory on morality. However, after one year he was summoned back to Edinburgh where, at the age of 19, he conducted his father's mathematical classes when his father fell ill, a position he maintained for 3 years, later succeeding his father to the chair of Mathematics at the University of Edinburgh in 1775 at 22 years of age.

As a young man he was influenced by, and corresponded regularly with, Lord Monboddo.

When Adam Ferguson was appointed secretary to the Commissioners sent to the American Colonies, Stewart lectured as his substitute and in addition to his lectures on mathematics, delivered an original course of lectures on morals in 1778–79.

Stewart was one of the last of the great figures of the Scottish Enlightenment, a lecturer in Moral Philosophy and Political Philosophy (and wrote many books on a variety of subjects) his classes attracting the finest young minds from all over Europe.

The Scottish Enlightenment was an intellectual movement that ranged across a wide variety of fields including philosophy, chemistry, geology, architecture, poetry, engineering, technology, economics, sociology, medicine and history.

Above: Dugald Stewart after Alexander Nasmyth

Below: View from Calton Hill

Enlightenment figures were outspoken and often controversial, arguing that it was important for people to think for themselves rather than simply accepting what they were told. Many historians believe that ideas that emerged from the Scottish Enlightenment helped to shape the modern world.

Above: Calton Hill

In 1785 Stewart succeeded Ferguson in the chair of Moral Philosophy. His reputation became worldwide; among his pupils were Lord Palmerston, Sir Walter Scott, Henry Cockburn, Sir James Macintosh and Sir Archibald Alison.

In August 1786, Dr MacKenzie sent him a copy of Burns' *Kilmarnock Edition* at his country home at Catrine, near Mauchline. He was so impressed by Burns' genius that he invited Burns to dine with him on 23rd October at Catrine.

Stewart paid a good deal of attention to Burns; Lord Cockburn said that *"Stewart supplied both young and old with philosophical ideas on what they had scarcely been accustomed to think philosophical subjects ... And that even his idler hearers retained a permanent taste for it."*

Below: Dugald Stewart Mausoleum

It was Stewart who first read Burns' *Kilmarnock Edition* to Dr Blacklock and wrote an account of his own first meeting with Burns.

Professor Dugald Stewart died in Edinburgh on 11th June 1828 in his 75th year. He is buried in the Canongate Kirkyard and Playfair's monument to his memory was erected on Calton Hill in 1832.

The Dugald Stewart building at the University of Edinburgh is in Charles Street and his portrait, by Raeburn, can be seen in the Scottish National Portrait Gallery.

Lines on Meeting with Lord Daer

This wot ye all whom it concerns,
I, Rhymer Robin, alias Burns,
October twenty-third,
A ne'er-to-be-forgotten day,
Sae far I sprackl'd up the brae,
I dinner'd wi' a Lord.

I've been at drucken writers' feasts,
Nay, been bitch-fou 'mang godly priests –
Wi' rev'rence be it spoken! –
I've even join'd the honour'd jorum,
When mighty Squireships of the quorum,
Their hydra drouth did sloken.

But wi' a Lord!-stand out my shin,
A Lord-a Peer-an Earl's son!
Up higher yet, my bonnet
An' sic a Lord! – lang Scotch ells twa,
Our Peerage he o'erlooks them a',
As I look o'er my sonnet.

But O for Hogarth's magic pow'r!
To show Sir Bardie's willyart glow'r,
An' how he star'd and stammer'd,
When, goavin, as if led wi' branks,
An' stumpin on his ploughman shanks,
He in the parlour hammer'd.

I sidying shelter'd in a nook,
An' at his Lordship steal't a look,
Like some portentous omen;
Except good sense and social glee,
An' (what surpris'd me) modesty,
I marked nought uncommon.

I watch'd the symptoms o' the Great,
The gentle pride, the lordly state,
The arrogant assuming;
The fient a pride, nae pride had he,
Nor sauce, nor state, that I could see,
Mair than an honest ploughman.

Then from his Lordship I shall learn,
Henceforth to meet with unconcern
One rank as weel's another;
Nae honest, worthy man need care
To meet with noble youthful Daer,
For he but meets a brother.

Burns Monument
Regent Road

With funds raised by public subscription, the statue of Robert Burns, which was originally housed inside this monument, is now to be seen at the Scottish National Portrait Gallery. However, the views of Edinburgh from the monument are well worth the short walk.

After Robert Burns died the idea of some sort of a Burns Monument was first proposed by Mr J. Forbes-Mitchell in Bombay in 1812. A subscription among expatriates was raised but despite amassing a large amount of money, there was little interest in the project.

A letter, dated 18th October 1817 from Sir James Shaw, held by the Robert Burns Birthplace Museum in Alloway, and recently transcribed by Jerry Brannigan, states that *"Forbes Mitchell and Mr Boswell of Auchinleck corresponded a considerable time ago about the appropriation of the Bombay money about £300."*

Kilmarnock-born Sir James was a past Lord Mayor of London and Member of Parliament and, as he was a major benefactor to the Burns' family after Robert's death, it is likely he was also the driving force in encouraging, and supporting, the committees for both the Ayrshire and Edinburgh monuments.

Above: John Forbes-Mitchell

Indeed it is recorded in the minutes dated 3rd October 1815, of the committee formed to conduct the subscription to build the monument at Alloway that *"The Committee observe, that Sir James Shaw of London, Bart., our Countryman, stands distinguished by the handsome Remittances the result of the Contributions, of his numerous and respectable London Friends, to whose exertions in support of the object of the Subscribers, the Admirers of the Bard are truly indebted."*

On the 3rd October 1815, the fund stood at £457; on the 9th October an additional list of subscribers as printed in the Ayr newspapers, *"on consequence of further Remittance from Sir Jas. Shaw"* meant the amount now stood at £518.

Shaw, being based in London, and with his contacts at the very highest level of London society and government, it is not surprising that a large meeting took place there on Saturday 5th June 1819 at the Freemason's Tavern under the chairmanship of the Grand Master Mason, the Duke of Sussex, sixth son of George III. A committee was formed to oversee subscription and the Duke of Atholl was voted as chairman.

John Flaxman was commissioned in July 1824 to produce a life-sized statue in marble. However, Flaxman died suddenly on 7th December 1826, the work being completed by his brother-in-law, Thomas Denman.

Sadly, Forbes-Mitchell died on 9th July 1822, like Flaxman, also never to see his work come to fruition.

Thomas Hamilton, the architect, was appointed to complete the Edinburgh monument. He had already designed the Burns Monument in Alloway and the nearby Royal High School in Edinburgh.

In a letter from London dated 18th October 1817, James Shaw writes that *"Mr Mitchell intimated his wish to erect a monument in Edinburgh"* adding that *"then it was to be in one of the new squares, or on Calton Hill ..."*

Hamilton said that as he was so honoured to be asked that he declined payment for the design work.

The interior painting was carried out by Robert Buchanan and the garden around was planted with flowers and shrubs mentioned in the poems and songs of Burns. Buchanan also declined payment for his work.

The foundation was laid on 8th September 1831 and from 1839 the monument was looked after by the City of Edinburgh. At this time it was suggested that the statue would have to be moved because of soot damage from the nearby gasworks.

It was moved eventually in 1846 to The University of Edinburgh Library, then to The Royal Scottish Academy in 1861, before coming to its present home in the Scottish National Portrait Gallery in 1889.

At the present time the monument and garden are normally closed, but can be viewed, for example, on Open Doors Day.

Left: Burns Monument

Sir James Shaw, Baronet

1764–1843 Lord Mayor of London

Regent Road

The son of an Ayrshire Farmer, John Shaw, James Shaw was born in Riccarton, near Kilmarnock, on 26th August 1764. His father died when Shaw was 5 years old and his mother moved the family to Kilmarnock.

Shaw attended Kilmarnock Grammar school. When he was 17 he moved to America to join his brother David and worked in the commercial house of George & Samuel Douglas of New York.

Three years later he moved to the company office in London, later becoming a partner.

Shaw was to live his life in London at 1 America Square in the heart of the city, involving himself in politics, becoming Lord Mayor of London in 1805, later being elected as a Member of Parliament for the City of London from 1806 to 1818.

In 1813, a notice dated April 15th, was placed in the *London Gazette*. It stated that *"The partnership of William Douglas, Baronet, Samuel Douglas, and Sir James Shaw, Bart, under the firm of Douglas and Shaw, of America Square, London, Merchants, being dissolved by the death of Sir William Douglas, and the retirement of Mr Samuel Douglas from the business, all debts due to, or by the concern, will be liquidated by the said Sir James Shaw."* Following this Sir James seems to have become a full-time politician.

After the death of Burns, Shaw became the single most important benefactor to the family, ensuring the boys first attended school in London before finding jobs for them. Through the direct intervention of Prime Minister Addington, Robert was found a position in the Stamp Office in London in 1804, and Shaw, using his position as a stockholder ensured the two youngest, James Glencairn and William Nicol, found positions (as lieutenants) in the East India Company, rising in rank to lieut. colonel and colonel respectively. Francis Wallace died of a fever at Dumfries in 1803 before he could take up the cadetship arranged by Shaw. He also arranged that Jean and the other children, including Burns' illegitimate daughters were cared for. In a letter Shaw stated, *"I have the pleasure to tell Jean Burnses sons are all provided for."*

Shaw was also involved at an early stage in the provision of funds for both the Alloway and Edinburgh monuments. He not only donated large sums of his own but he encouraged many subscriptions from fellow politicians and others in public life, none more important than the Prince Regent.

It is thought that Shaw could have owned a copy of of Nasmyth's portrait of Burns. The name "Shaw" is written in pencil on the strainer at the rear of the painting. This lay undiscovered for many years until purchased at a provincial

Above: Sir James Shaw

sale in England in 2011. There was a two-year examination by experts including infrared and x-ray before the painting was authenticated as the work of Alexander Nasmyth.

Shaw was a great patron of the arts and his rooms were 'crowded with paintings of those in his patronising care.' However, when he died, no paintings were left to London Corporation as specified in his will. He was elected Chamberlain of London in 1831 and inadvertently invested £40,000 for London Corporation in forged Exchequer notes. This was a significant sum then, equivalent to over £3,000,000 today. He vowed to make good the loss and used his own fortune and assets, leaving him with few funds. It is thought that his collection of paintings were sold at this time. Later, a Government Commission exonerated Shaw from any wrongdoing and repaid the full amount of money.

A public subscription raised £1,000 to cover the cost of a memorial to Shaw, and a statue by James Fillans was erected to Shaw in Kilmarnock town centre in 1848. The inauguration of the statue was attended by all the great and the good of the area and with full Masonic honours. The ceremony was attended by thousands of citizens of Kilmarnock. In 1929 the statue was moved to the Dick Institute in the town.

Sir James took ill in May 1843, and died on 22nd October of the same year in his house at 1 America Square in London.

Sir James Shaw never married; his nephew John MacGee, took the baronetcy and changed his name to Shaw, being known as Sir John Shaw. His nephew also died unmarried and childless, the title becoming extinct.

Left: Sir James Shaw statue

Canongate

1. Kirk of the Canongate
2. St John Street
3. St Patrick's Church
4. St Cecilia's Hall

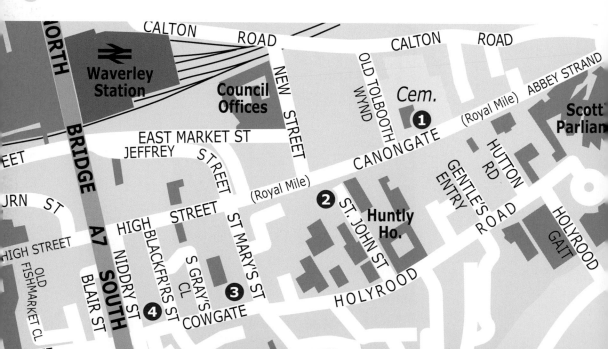

Kirk of the Canongate
153 Canongate, EH8 8BN

Robert Burns himself commissioned the gravestone for fellow poet, Robert Fergusson. On the opposite side of the kirkyard is buried his Clarinda, Agnes McLehose.

Below: Kirk of the Canongate

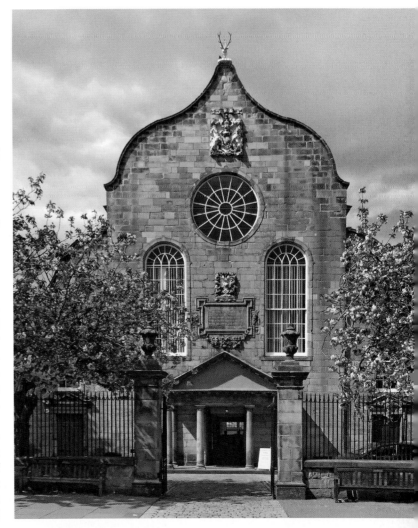

King James VII ordered the construction of this kirk (church) in 1691 while he was converting the Abbey Kirk at the Palace of Holyroodhouse, also known as Holyrood Palace, into a chapel for the Order of the Thistle. This is the parish church of Edinburgh Castle and the Palace of Holyroodhouse, pews being reserved for the Royal Family.

Portraits of the monarchs of the day are displayed in the nearby World's End pub (so called because it was at the gates of the ancient city of Edinburgh).

Agnes McLehose frequented this kirk and is buried on the east side of the kirkyard alongside her cousin Lord William Craig. On the wall above her grave is an engraving of Agnes based on the famous silhouette commissioned by Burns, and made by Miers.

On the left side (west) of the kirk is one of the most important memorials in Edinburgh; that of Burns to his fellow poet, Robert Fergusson. It was Robert Burns who had the headstone erected over Fergusson's unmarked grave, commissioning the architect Robert Burn to carry out the work. The rear of the stone records that it was erected by Burns.

Other prominent Edinburgh figures buried here: Dugald Stewart, Professor

Above: The grave of Agnes McLehose (Clarinda)

Above, right: The Burns Monument, seen from Clarinda's grave

of Moral Philosophy; The Reverend Robert Walker (subject of the portrait *The Skating Minister*); Adam Smith, the philosopher and economist and Alexander Runciman, the painter.

David Rizzio, private secretary to Mary Queen of Scots (Mary I of Scotland), is also alleged to be buried here on the east side of the church building, although as a Catholic, it is unlikely. Rizzio was an Italian musician and singer who managed to ingratiate himself into the group of musicians surrounding the queen. When Rizzio, a foreigner and a Catholic, became Mary's private secretary this caused disquiet about his closeness to the queen. Rumours about an affair circulated and he was murdered, being stabbed 56 times, in front of the heavily pregnant Mary, in her private dining room in the Palace of Holyroodhouse, on 9th March 1566.

The Kirk of the Canongate
153 Canongate, Edinburgh, EH8 8BN
0131 556 3515
www.canongatekirk.org.uk

Robert Fergusson
1750–74 Poet

Robert Fergusson was born in Edinburgh on 5th September 1750, just off the High Street. He was educated at the University of St Andrews, but failed to complete his studies and eventually found work as a copyist, making copies of other authors' manuscripts.

He was very sociable and mixed with many of Edinburgh's literati. He often visited the Theatre Royal. His friend, the actor William Woods, supplied him with free tickets. Fergusson even wrote songs for an opera which was staged in the Theatre Royal.

From 1771 he wrote and published poems, many of them in Scots, the language of Scotland, recently usurped by English because of the Union of Parliaments. In 1773, 500 copies of his poetic works were sold and Burns read one in 1781. The long poem, *Auld Reekie*, published later, is regarded as his masterpiece. It is a magnificent description of Edinburgh and its citizens, called 'reekie' because, as Boswell and Creech have recorded, it stank. (Reek is an old Scots word meaning smell.)

Like Burns, Fergusson frequented clubs such as the one at Craig's Close, the Cape Club, reputed to be patronised by the notorious Deacon Brodie, cabinet-maker and city councillor by day and burglar by night, who lived near the pub which now bears his name. Other members of the club were the artists Sir Henry Racburn and Alexander Runciman. The club's minute book is housed in the National Library of Scotland, George IV Bridge.

Above: Robert Fergusson (after Alexander Runciman)

Burns was a very disciplined man, but Fergusson, sadly, was not. He drank a lot. Like Burns, Fergusson suffered from melancholy, but Fergusson's was of a different degree. In 1774, he was admitted to the aptly named Bedlam Hospital, an asylum which was situated behind the present day Bedlam Theatre at the end of George IV Bridge. This building adjoined a workhouse for the poor and was constructed around 1698; it was Scotland's first purpose-built asylum.

Fergusson died after a fall down stairs only a few weeks later on 16th October 1774, aged only 24. When his last hours came, *"his piteous shrieks for his 'mother' often rang out upon the night".*

When Burns visited the churchyard, he was saddened that no stone marked the grave of one of his favourite poets. Burns requested permission from the Governors of Edinburgh's Canongate Kirk, to erect a monument to Fergusson. This was granted and Burns engaged Robert Burn, the architect, to design and install the monumental stone. Burn sent Burns the following note: *"I shall be glad to receive orders of the like nature for as many of your friends that have gone hence as you please."*

Burns was tardy in settling his account with Burn, finally sending payment via Peter Hill. In a letter from Dumfries on the 5th February 1792 Burns writes, *"… five pounds ten shillings per account I owe Mr R. Burn, architect, for erecting the stone over the grave of poor Fergusson. He was two years in erecting it after I had commissioned him for it, and I have been two years in paying him, after he sent me his account; so he and I are quits. He had the hardiesse to ask me interest on the sum; but, considering that the money was due by one poet for putting a tombstone over another, he may, with grateful surprise, thank Heaven that he ever saw a farthing of it."*

Yet another Robert is associated with the monument: Robert Louis Stevenson. He noted that its condition was deteriorating and wished to upgrade it, but he died before he could manage this. The restoration was, however, finally carried out in 2009 in a partnership between the Edinburgh Burns Club, the Robert Louis Stevenson Club and Scottish Government.

A recent memorial to Fergusson is to be seen at the entrance to the Kirk in the form of a statue of Fergusson, erected by the Burns Society of New York and the St Andrew's Society of New York.

Right: Beside the front gate to the Kirk of the Canongate stands David Annand's sculpture of Robert Fergusson, unveiled in 2004.

Here Lies Robert Fergusson, Poet

No sculptur'd marble here, nor pompous lay,
No story'd urn nor animated bust;
This simple stone directs pale Scotia's way
To pour her sorrows o'er her Poet's dust.

She mourns, sweet, tuneful youth, thy hapless fate,
Tho' all the pow'rs of song thy fancy fir'd;
Yet Luxury and Wealth lay by in state,
And thankless starv'd what they so much admir'd.

This humble tribute with a tear he gives,
A brother Bard, he can no more bestow;
But dear to fame thy Song immortal lives,
A nobler monument than Art can show.

Below, left: Robert Fergusson headstone front (above) and rear (below)

Below: The grave in Canongate Kirkyard.

John Campbell
1750–95 Singer

Above: John Campbell

Below: Giusto Tenducci

A precentor (from the Latin meaning, one who sings before) is someone who leads worship. John Campbell was Precentor of Canongate Church for 20 years.

He was born in the family home of the village of Tombea, 20 miles northwest of Callander, Perthshire, in 1750, but the family savings were lost when the laird of the estate was made bankrupt. His father moved the family to Edinburgh, but died suddenly soon after, leaving John, now 20 years old, to provide for the family.

He took unskilled work as a woodcutter and, at the same time, gained such a reputation as an amateur vocalist that the Reverend Robert Walker recommended him to Reverend MacFarlane who made him Precentor of the Canongate Church in 1775. He then had singing lessons from the celebrated Italian Soprano, Giusto Tenducci, whom John impressed so much that on leaving Edinburgh Tenducci passed notes of recommendation to his social and celebrity acquaintances ensuring that John Campbell and his brother had enough custom to teach professionally.

Campbell said that Burns would drop in of an evening and drink tea for an hour or so before rushing away to *"become the lion of some fashionable party or to join the deep carousal of a tavern debauch"*.

It was to Campbell that Burns turned to when he decided to put a memorial over the grave of Fergusson. Campbell took Burns to see Bailie Gentle who expressed doubts that the committee would agree. Burns said, *"Tell them it is the Ayrshire ploughman who makes the request."*

It was also Campbell who facilitated the introduction of Burns to the renowned Architect, Robert Burn, who agreed to carry out the work.

The cartoon of Campbell by the famous caricaturist James Gillray is titled: *"Mr J___ C___, the Jolly Precentor of the Canongate Kirk, in Edinburgh, Singing Psalms of a Morning and Over a Bowl of Punch, Scotch Tunes at Night."*

In other words just the sort of person Burns would spend time with, and indeed Burns was a frequent visitor to his home.

Reverend Robert Walker

1755–1808 Minister

Walker was born in Monkton, Ayrshire, only a few miles from Burns' birthplace and barely 4 years later. In 1784 he was *"called to the vacancy"* of the post of senior minister in the Kirk of the Canongate. A family connection existed with the Kirk as Walker's grandfather had been minister there 40 years previously.

He married Jean Fraser, the daughter of an Edinburgh lawyer.

He was a member of the Royal Company of Archers in 1779 and was their chaplain from 1798 to 1808.

Robert Burns' Edinburgh publisher William Creech was a friend of Walker's and published a book of his sermons in 1791.

Walker is most famous, though, because he is the subject of Sir Henry Raeburn's painting *The Reverend Walker Skating on Duddingston Loch* which is more popularly known as *The Skating Minister.* The painting can be seen in the National Gallery of Scotland on the Mound. Walker was a keen skater having learnt the skill as a child while in Holland where his father was minister of the Scots Kirk in Rotterdam.

Above: Reverend Robert Walker

It was natural then that he should join the Edinburgh Skating Club, which was the world's first figure skating club (formed in 1742).

In March 2005, following research, a suggestion was made that the painting was not in fact by Raeburn, but by the French artist Henri-Pierre Danloux.

Danloux was probably in Edinburgh during the 1790s, when *The Skating Minister* was painted. Reports indicate that the canvas and scale of the painting do seem to be that of a French painter, although Raeburn critics disagree.

Walker is buried within the Canongate Kirkyard, but sadly the location of his grave is not known.

St John Street
EH8 8DG

At the head of the street is Lodge Canongate Kilwinning No. 2, the building where Burns was celebrated as Scotland's Poet Laureate. Also in this street was the home of Lord Monboddo where Burns was first introduced to Scotland's finest academics and writers.

Through the pend marked St John Street, just off the Canongate, you will find what must rank as the most influential street of 18th-century Edinburgh. Robert Burns would have walked here very regularly.

St John's Cross marked the boundary of the Burgh of Canongate and the steps to the Cross were used as a meeting place for magistrates, constables, traders and for reading out proclamations.

Traditionally, visiting royalty were greeted here by the Provosts of Edinburgh and Canongate. On this spot in 1617, James VI knighted William Nisbet, Provost of Edinburgh and in 1633, Charles I, on a ceremonial entry into the city, knighted the provost here.

In 1987 the site of the Cross was marked out on the roadway on Canongate, just outside of the pend.

In the mid-1700s, before the rich and famous began their move to the New Town, St John Street was occupied by the very wealthy. The terrace of tenements on the east side had many aristocratic and influential residents: No. 2 The Earl of Aboyne; No. 3 Lord Ballantyne; No. 4 The Earl of Dalhousie; No. 5 Dr Gregory; No. 8 The Earl of Hyndford; No. 11 Elizabeth Wemyss; No. 12 Colonel Todd; No. 13 Lord Monboddo and his daughter Elizabeth.

Below, left: St John Street today

Below, right: St John Street as it was in Burns' time

Left: St John Street

A plaque on the inside of the close informs us that the author Tobias Smollett (1721–71) lived here at No. 22 in 1766.

No. 1 was the home of the street porter. His job was to bar access to any vehicle and also *'to prevent any carpet beating in the close outside restricted hours'*. Other duties included sweeping the street at least once a day and 'prevent children and idlers from lounging on the stairs, destroying the fence or in any way annoying the neighbours'.

This is where Monboddo regularly held his 'learned suppers' attracting the finest minds, and celebrities, who found their way to Scotland's capital.

The Masonic Lodge, Canongate Kilwinning No. 2 was almost opposite Monboddo's house. It was here that Burns attended Masonic meetings and was recognised as Scotland's Poet Laureate by the Grand Lodge of Scotland.

Lodge Canongate Kilwinning No. 2

The Lodge was formerly known as St John's Lodge, Canongate because of its location, but its correct name is Lodge Canongate Kilwinning No. 2. The masons in the Canongate obtained a charter from the Mother Lodge of Scotland at Kilwinning in 1677. Built in 1672, with additions in 1735, it is the oldest purpose-built Masonic Temple in the world. It exists today largely as it was constructed and is still used by the Lodge for its meetings.

Below: Interior, Lodge Canongate Kilwinning No. 2

Bottom: Francis Charteris

Robert Burns certainly attended here. At a meeting of Lodge Canongate Kilwinning No. 2 in Edinburgh on Thursday 1st February 1787, Robert Burns was assumed a member of the Lodge as recorded in the minutes: *"The RW Master having observed that Brother Burns was at present in the Lodge, who is well known as a great poetic writer, and for a late publication of his works, which have been universally commended, submitted that he should be assumed a member of this Lodge, which was unanimously agreed to and he was assumed accordingly."*

It was here, in this building, that Robert Burns was lauded as Caledonia's Bard by the Grand Master Mason of Scotland, Bro. the Hon. Francis Charteris and The Grand Lodge of Scotland believed to be at a meeting of Lodge St Andrews on 13th January 1787.

Tradition has it that on Thursday 1st March, Burns was installed as Poet Laureate of the Lodge by Canongate Kilwinning No. 2.

According to the painting, which can be viewed in the Freemasons' Hall Museum, this was a huge occasion with 60 members identified. This meeting with the Grand Master Mason and all, did not appear in minutes, and was not recorded elsewhere, creating no small amount of controversy.

In 1754, Johan Snetzler, one of Europe's foremost organ makers based in London, visited Edinburgh and provided an estimate of £70 for an organ to complete the Masonic Chapel of St John. It is said that in London the organ was appraised and played by Handel before being sent by sea to Leith and transported to Edinburgh by cart.

The organ has been in regular use since its installation on 4th August 1757, with original pipes, mechanism, case etc and is still pumped by hand. Owing to its size, a section of the rear wall had to be opened up to bring the organ into the chapel. This is now the alcove near the doorway.

Below: Mural, Lodge Canongate Kilwinning No. 2

Bottom: William St Clair

William St Clair of Roslin (1700–78) was, in 1736, the first ever Grand Master Mason of Scotland shortly after becoming Master of Lodge Canongate Kilwinning No. 2. There are portraits of him both in Archers' Hall and in the Lodge. His family are the famous St Clairs, described in *The Da Vinci Code,* who built the magnificent Rosslyn Chapel in 1466.

The vast majority of those with influence and power in Edinburgh in the 18th century were Freemasons, and attended the Lodge.

Other famous members of the Lodge include:

Allan Masterton (c1750–99), musician; Girolamo Stabilini (c1762–1815), violinist and composer, leader of St Cecilia's Hall; Louis Cauvin, the French teacher of Burns, John Beugo, and Stephen Clarke. Louis Cauvin built the charitable Cauvin's Hospital

in Willowbrae Avenue; Stephen Clarke, Organist at St Paul's Episcopal Church in Cowgate, now St Patrick's RC Church, and also a composer for the *Scots Musical Museum*; William Cruikshank, Burns' landlord in St James Square; Johann Georg Christof Schetky, composer of *Clarinda, Mistress of my Soul*; James 'Balloon' Tytler (c1747–1803), the first Scottish balloonist and the first man in Britain to fly.

Lodge Canongate Kilwinning No. 2
23 St John Street
Edinburgh
EH8 8DG
secretary@lck2.co.uk
www.lck2.co.uk

Below: Interior, Lodge Canongate Kilwinning No. 2

James Cunningham
14th Earl of Glencairn, Lord Kilmaurs
1749–81 Burns' Patron

James Cunningham was born at born at Finlaystone House, Langbank, Renfrewshire on the 1st June 1749.

From 1780–84 he was one of the representative Scots peers in the House of Lords. He was the key to Burns' success.

Glencairn and his mother subscribed to 24 copies of the *Kilmarnock Edition*. When Burns arrived in Edinburgh armed with letters of introduction from Dalrymple of Orangefield, who was married to Glencairn's sister, the earl received him warmly and introduced Burns to his friends.

One of these, Henry Erskine of the Faculty of Advocates, introduced Burns to Jane Maxwell, Duchess of Gordon. Glencairn also introduced Burns to William Creech who had been Glencairn's tutor and travelling companion, and who was to become Burns' publisher of the *Edinburgh Editions* of Burns' book, *Poems Chiefly in the Scottish Dialect*.

Burns corresponded regularly with Glencairn valuing greatly his friendship and advice, referring to Glencairn as his 'Titular Protector'.

The *Edinburgh Editions* were dedicated to the Caledonian Hunt – an exclusive body of *"persons of first distinction in Scotland"* who shared a common interest in field sports, races, and social assemblies. The annual Hunters Ball was the highlight of the Edinburgh social calendar with invitations being much sought after. In acknowledgement of this, Glencairn made a motion on 10th January 1787 that, in consideration of Burns' superior merit, the Caledonian Hunt should subscribe for 100 copies in their name. Burns was enrolled as a member of the Caledonian Hunt on 16th April 1792.

Above: James Cunningham

In January 1788, Burns wrote to Glencairn asking for his assistance in finding him an appointment with the Excise.

Glencairn never enjoyed good health, travelling to winter in the sunnier climes of Lisbon in 1790, but returning early in January 1791. He never married. He died in Falmouth on 30th January 1791, aged 42, from tuberculosis, soon after arriving from the continent and is buried in the Church of King Charles the Martyr in Falmouth.

His brother John succeeded him in the title as the 15th Earl of Glencairn, and Burns wrote in 1793, enclosing a copy of the newly published *Edinburgh Edition*. It was a letter of introduction, and an acknowledgment of the esteem that Burns still held for John's late brother.

Burns wrote, *"The generous patronage of your late illustrious brother found me in the utmost obscurity: he introduced my rustic muse to the partiality of my country; and to him I owe all. My sense of his goodness and the anguish of my soul at losing my truly noble protector and friend I have endeavoured to express in a poem to his memory, which I have now published."*

In memory of the earl, Burns named his fourth son James Glencairn Burns.

Lament for James, Earl of Glencairn

The wind blew hollow frae the hills,
By fits the sun's departing beam
Look'd on the fading yellow woods
That wav'd o'er Lugar's winding stream:
Beneath a craigy steep, a Bard,
Laden with years and meikle pain,
In loud lament bewail'd his lord,
Whom Death had all untimely ta'en.

He lean'd him to an ancient aik,
Whose trunk was mould'ring down with years;
His locks were bleached white with time,
His hoary cheek was wet wi' tears;
And as he touch'd his trembling harp,
And as he tun'd his doleful sang,
The winds, lamenting thro' their caves,
To Echo bore the notes alang.

"Ye scatter'd birds that faintly sing,
The reliques o' the vernal queir;
Ye woods that shed on a' the winds
The honours of the aged year:
A few short months, and glad and gay,
Again ye'll charm the ear and e'e;
But nocht in all-revolving time
Can gladness bring again to me.

"I am a bending aged tree,
That long has stood the wind and rain;
But now has come a cruel blast,
And my last hald of earth is gane;
Nae leaf o' mine shall greet the spring,
Nae simmer sun exalt my bloom;
But I maun lie before the storm,
And ithers plant them in my room.

"I've seen sae mony changefu' years,
On earth I am a stranger grown;
I wander in the ways of men,
Alike unknowing, and unknown:
Unheard, unpitied, unreliev'd,
I bear alane my lade o' care,
For silent, low, on beds of dust,
Lie a' that would my sorrows share.

"And last, (the sum of a' my griefs!)
My noble master lies in clay;
The flow'r amang our barons bold,
His country's pride, his country's stay:
In weary being now I pine,
For a' the life of life is dead,
And hope has left my aged ken,
On forward wing for ever fled.

"Awake thy last sad voice, my harp!
The voice of woe and wild despair!
Awake, resound thy latest lay,
Then sleep in silence evermair!
And thou, my last, best, only, friend,
That fillest an untimely tomb,
Accept this tribute from the Bard
Thou brought from Fortune's mirkest gloom.

"In Poverty's low barren vale,
Thick mists obscure involv'd me round;
Though oft I turn'd the wistful eye,
Nae ray of fame was to be found:
Thou found'st me, like the morning sun
That melts the fogs in limpid air,
The friendless bard and rustic song,
Became alike thy fostering care.

"O! why has Worth so short a date?
While villains ripen grey with time!
Must thou, the noble, gen'rous, great,
Fall in bold manhood's hardy prime!
Why did I live to see that day?
A day to me so full of woe?
O! had I met the mortal shaft
That laid my benefactor low!

"The bridegroom may forget the bride,
Was made his wedded wife yestreen;
The monarch may forget the crown
That on his head an hour has been;
The mother may forget the child
That smiles sae sweetly on her knee;
But I'll remember thee, Glencairn,
And a' that thou hast done for me!"

James Burnett, Lord Monboddo

1714–99 Lawyer

Through his parties, called 'learned suppers' James Burnett facilitated a number of significant connections for Robert Burns

James Burnett was born on his father's estate at Monboddo House, Kincardineshire on 25th October 1714.

Monboddo attended Edinburgh University and Groningen University in the Netherlands, studying Greek, philosophy and law. He was called to the bar (became a lawyer) in 1737. When he became a judge in the Court of Session in 1767 he took the title of Lord Monboddo.

Monboddo was renowned for his *"learned suppers"*, at 13 St John Street, inviting the most influential in science, art, and literature with a plentiful supply of his favourite claret ensuring lively discussion. Burns was a welcome guest here on several occasions and he would have met many of Edinburgh's most important people here, including the poet Alison Cockburn.

As a young lawyer he was involved in the 'Douglas Cause'. This celebrated inheritance dispute involved litigation, in Scotland, France and England, stories of stolen babies, lawyers fighting duels with each other, culminating in two days of rioting on the streets of Edinburgh. The young Monboddo was part of the victorious legal team. It is thought that the father of Louis Cauvin (Burns' French language teacher in Edinburgh) may have come to Scotland to give evidence in the Scottish court as he had been involved with one of the parties in France.

Below: Lord Monboddo

Monboddo was a prolific writer and produced books on such diverse subjects as the origin of language and ancient metaphysics. While his views were regarded as rather extreme and eccentric, some scholars considered Monboddo to have developed the concepts of evolution 70 years before Darwin.

He studied language in great detail, being proficient in ancient Greek which he regarded as the most perfect of languages. He also studied such diverse languages as Huron, Peruvian, Eskimo, Tahitian and wrote a treatise on Chinese.

An eccentric, both in character and appearance, Monboddo was captured on several occasions by the caricaturist John Kay.

When Burns arrived in Edinburgh, Monboddo had recently fallen out with his friend James Boswell, the biographer of Samuel Johnson. Sadly Burns was never to meet Boswell.

Burns was very taken with Monboddo's daughter Elizabeth, and was very upset at her early death, writing an *Elegy on The Late Miss Burnet of Monboddo*.

James Burnett, Lord Monboddo died on 26th May 1799 in his 85th year, and is buried in the family crypt in Greyfriars Kirkyard.

Elizabeth (Bess) Burnett
1766–90 Friend, daughter of James

Elizabeth was Monboddo's second daughter and 20 years old when she met Burns. She was a renowned beauty and was the first woman in Edinburgh to turn his head. He remarked in a letter, *"There has not been anything nearly like her ... since Milton's Eve on the first day of her existence."*

The poet, Alison Cockburn said of Burns *"he has seen Duchess of Gordon and all the gay world. His favourite for looks and manners is Bess Burnet, no bad judge indeed!"*

Burns included her in his *Address to Edinburgh* and composed an elegy to her after she died.

Tragically, she died of tuberculosis, aged 25, at Braid Farm, near Edinburgh. She is buried in Greyfriars Kirkyard alongside her father.

Above: Elizabeth Burnett Monboddo

Elegy On The Late Miss Burnet Of Monboddo

Life ne'er exulted in so rich a prize,
As Burnet, lovely from her native skies;
Nor envious death so triumph'd in a blow,
As that which laid th' accomplish'd Burnet low.

Thy form and mind, sweet maid, can I forget?
In richest ore the brightest jewel set!
In thee, high Heaven above was truest shown,
As by His noblest work the Godhead best is known.

In vain ye flaunt in summer's pride, ye groves;
Thou crystal streamlet with thy flowery shore,
Ye woodland choir that chaunt your idle loves,
Ye cease to charm; Eliza is no more.

Ye healthy wastes, immix'd with reedy fens;
Ye mossy streams, with sedge and rushes stor'd:
Ye rugged cliffs, o'erhanging dreary glens,
To you I fly – ye with my soul accord.

Princes, whose cumb'rous pride was all their worth,
Shall venal lays their pompous exit hail,
And thou, sweet Exccllence! forsake our earth,
And not a Muse with honest grief bewail?

We saw thee shine in youth and beauty's pride,
And Virtue's light, that beams beyond the spheres;
But, like the sun eclips'd at morning tide,
Thou left us darkling in a world of tears.

The parent's heart that nestled fond in thee,
That heart how sunk, a prey to grief and care;
So deckt the woodbine sweet yon aged tree;
So, rudely ravish'd, left it bleak and bare.

Henry Erskine
1746–1817 Lord Advocate

Above: Henry Erskine

Erskine was the second son of the 10th Earl of Buchan. He was called to the bar in 1768 later becoming Lord Advocate, being called to the role twice, in 1783 and 1806.

Burns wrote about him in *Extempore in the Court of Session*. Erskine was a leader of the reform movement in Edinburgh and a member of the Crochallan Fencibles, one of a number of Edinburgh's convivial clubs. Burns would have met him at the Fencibles where he would enjoy Erskine's renowned debating skill and would become his literal sparring partner.

The Crochallan Fencibles was mainly a drinking club but may have also been a meeting place for those with Jacobite sympathies. Burns wrote many bawdy songs to be sung in the club and these were published after his death under the auspices of the Fencibles.

Erskine had also been a Past Master of Lodge Canongate Kilwinning No. 2 and Burns became apprentice there on 1st February 1787. In a letter to Gavin Hamilton in Mauchline, Burns writes, *"My Lord Glencairn and the Dean of Faculty, Mr H. Erskine, have taken me under their wing; and by all probability I shall soon be the tenth worthy, and the eighth wise man of the world."*

Henry Erskine died on 8th October 1817, aged 70, and is buried in the churchyard of St Nicholas, Uphall.

Extempore in the Court of Session

Lord Advocate

He clench'd his pamphlets in his fist,
He quoted and he hinted,
Till in a declamation-mist,
His argument he tint it:
He gaped for 't, he graped for 't,
He fand it was awa, man;
And what his common sense came short,
He eked out wi' law, man.

Mr Erskine

Collected, Harry stood awee,
Then open'd out his arm, man;
His lordship sat wi' ruefu' e'e,
And ey'd the gathering storm, man:
Like wind-driv'n hail it did assail,
Or torrents owre a lin, man;
The bench sae wise lift up their eyes,
Half-wauken'd wi' the din, man.

James Tytler
1745–1804 Balloonist

James Tytler was born in Fern, near Brechin on the 17th December 1745. He made aviation history by becoming the first person in Britain to make a manned ascent in a flying machine, the country's first aeronaut!

Tytler had a great interest in music, and was proficient in playing the Irish bagpipes, composing many melodies for the instrument. When Robert Burns was engaged by James Johnson to edit the second volume of the *Scots Musical Museum*, he recruited Tytler to assist him. Tytler himself contributed several songs to the volume. Burns may have met him at a Freemason's meeting as Tytler was a member at Lodge Canongate Killwinning No. 2.

Burns said of Tytler, *"commonly known by the name of Balloon Tytler from having projected a balloon; a mortal who trudges about Edinburgh as a common printer, with leaky shoes, and sky-lighted hat … yet that same unknown, drunken mortal is author and compiler of three-fourths of Elliot's pompous* Encyclopaedia Britannica *which he composed at half a guinea a week."*

"Pompous" as used in Burns' description meant "magnificent" at this time. Indeed Burns regarded the *Encyclopaedia* so highly that he arranged with William Creech to exchange 58 copies of the *Edinburgh Edition* for 10 volumes of the encyclopaedia.

Above: James Tytler

The son of a Presbyterian minister, Tytler was taught Greek, Latin and theology by his father, becoming a preacher for a time in the Church of Scotland. After studying medicine at the University of Edinburgh he apprenticed as a ship's surgeon working on a whaling ship, a job that lasted only a year. He didn't practice medicine after this but opened a pharmacy in Leith, a financially disastrous undertaking which left him in much debt.

In 1765 he married Elizabeth Rattray, but soon after both had to flee to Newcastle to escape creditors, where he again tried to make a living as an apothecary. This was also a

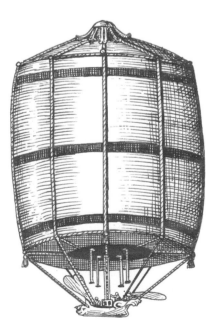

Left, inset: Tytler's Great Edinburgh Fire Balloon

failure and in 1772 he returned to Edinburgh and attempted to make a living as a writer. He was a prolific writer of many types of publications, including very early geographical magazines, but could not earn enough to support his family and again had to seek refuge from creditors in the Debtors' Sanctuary of Holyrood House.

The book, *Rangers Impartial List of the Ladies of Pleasure in Edinburgh (with Preface by a Celebrated Wit)* published in 1775 as a guide to prostitutes of the city, was thought to have been compiled by Tytler, as were many other anonymously published books and leaflets, most likely published on printing machines that he built by hand during his stay in the Debtors' Sanctuary.

Beset by alcoholism and still unable to generate a living, he and Elizabeth separated, leaving her to look after their 5 children.

Above: Debtors' Sanctuary. Abbey Strand, the shortest section of the Royal Mile, runs to the gates of the Palace of Holyrood House.

In 1777 he edited the second edition of the Encyclopaedia Britannica, which was being printed in Edinburgh. This was steady and regular work though he was paid only 16 shillings a week, much less than William Smellie, the previous editor. Other editing and translation work helped to sustain him. The work on the encyclopaedia was very suited to Tytler and his wealth of knowledge in a huge variety of subjects. Almost single-handedly he enlarged the original edition from 3 to 10 volumes, and this may have sparked his interest in ballooning.

When the work on the second edition finished in 1784, he then turned to hot-air ballooning. His knowledge of chemistry, along with what he had learned from the encyclopaedia, led him to design and build his own balloon, an expensive endeavour.

In an effort to raise some funds, Tytler constructed a 13-foot high model, exhibiting it in Comely Gardens, charging the public sixpence to view his Great Edinburgh Fire Balloon. When he had completed construction of the full-sized balloon, this was inflated and tested in the partly completed Register House at the eastern end of Princes Stret, the domed roof being a perfect fit for the 40-foot-high balloon. Today, Tytler Gardens and Tytler Court, to the east of Holyroodhouse, lie on the site of Comely Gardens.

An attempt on 6th August to fly the balloon failed. Tytler was attacked by the press, while the balloon was attacked by the crowd.

On 25th August 1784 his balloon rose a few feet from the ground, and *The Edinburgh Courant* noted that "*it fairly floated*". Two days later, on 27th August 1784 the balloon rose to a height of some 350 feet, travelling half-a-mile to come to rest in the village of Restalrig.

On the 31st he made a third flight but crashed in front of hundreds of paying spectators. He was now known by the name 'Balloon' Tytler and the first man in Britain to fly, securing a place in the history of aviation.

Unfortunately Tytler may have had a head for heights, but not for business and was unable to turn his invention and experience to profit.

In contrast, the Lunardi brothers came to Scotland the following year with their flying balloon show, and the extravaganza attracted 80,000 people who gathered on Heriot's Hospital Green to watch.

Shortly afterwards in 1785 Tytler was again made bankrupt and had to move around Scotland and northern England, enduring another period at the Debtors' Sanctuary in Holyrood.

The Debtors' Sanctuary, more correctly called Abbey Sanctuary, was an area of around 5 miles in circumference, taking in the whole of Holyrood Park, where those in debt could escape their creditors and often violent retribution or long periods of imprisonment. A community grew up in this area to the west of the palace and 'residents' were known as Abbey Lairds.

The debtor had to make an application to the Bailie of Holyrood and on acceptance, and payment of the 2-guinea fee, was issued with papers of protection. The area was policed by the bailie and his constables, who in the present day constitute a ceremonial guard.

The boundary of the Sanctuary is marked by the letter S, visible in the roadway at Abbey Strand. On a Sunday, the debtor was allowed to cross the boundary without fear of arrest as no legal proceedings took place on that day.

Tytler built a printing press in the sanctuary and it was here that he printed various pamphlets as well as his political leaflets.

By this time he was living with Jean Aitkenhead, having had twin girls with her, and Elizabeth sued him for divorce.

In 1788 he started work on the third edition of the *Encyclopaedia Brittanica*, and this gave him a regular, but low income for the next 5 years.

Tytler was always interested in politics, having being born in the year of the failed '45 Rebellion and the years that followed stoked the fires of his nationalism. The publishers of the encyclopaedia, Bell and MacFarquar, restrained any outspoken articles from Tytler within its pages, but Tytler published A Pamphlet on the Excise and The Historical Register. A Handbill Addressed to the People followed in which he expressed sympathy for the French Revolution, and claimed the House of Commons was robbing both king and people, and called on the British people to withhold taxes.

He also stated that voting should be a right for every upright and honest citizen and not a preserve of the rich. This was at a time when Thomas Muir and the political martyrs were being brought to trial in Edinburgh for similar views on political reform. In 1793 Tytler was charged with seditious libel by the Scottish Courts, forcing him to flee first to Belfast and then to the United States. He ended up in Salem, Massachusetts, earning a small income with some writing work, selling medicines and editing the local *Salem Register*.

His problem with alcohol never went away and on 9th January 1804, in a drunken state, he left his house during a thunderstorm and was drowned, aged 58, after falling into a flooded clay pit.

Below: Debtors' Sanctuary boundary

Below: Vincent Lunardi

Rev Bishop John Geddes

1735–99 Friend

Bishop John Geddes was ordained a priest 18th March 1759, and became Bishop of Dunkeld on 30th November 1780.

Above: Bishop John Geddes

Burns was very friendly with this Roman Catholic bishop whom he met at one of Lord Monboddo's 'learned gatherings'. At this period in Scottish history, it was perhaps unwise for a Catholic of standing to have such a high public profile when only a few years earlier Bishop Hay's chapel house on Leith Wynd had been destroyed and set ablaze by a mob while the authorities looked on. Geddes' plan though, was to try to influence the opinion-formers of 18th century Scotland – and they were certainly to be found in Monboddo's company.

As well as caring for the Catholics of Edinburgh, Bishop Geddes would walk every 6 weeks or so to Glasgow to attend on the 60 Catholics who resided in the city.

Geddes immediately took an interest in Burns' work, writing to a fellow priest on 26th March 1787 that, *"he has made many poems in old Scotch … he is in town just now and I supped with him at Lord Monboddo's where I conversed a good deal with him, and think him a man of uncommon genius; and he has, as yet, if he lives, to cultivate it."*

In one of his many letters to her, Burns wrote to Mrs Dunlop of Dunlop about Geddes, writing that the finest cleric character he ever saw was a Roman Catholic, a *"Popish Bishop, Geddes"*.

Geddes and Burns corresponded several times, with many of their letters surviving, and it is clear that they had formed a mutual respect, Geddes encouraging 5 Catholic seminaries to subscribe to the *Edinburgh Edition* of 1787.

Burns took Geddes' copy with him on his Highland tour but it was almost 2 years before he returned it, apologising in a letter from Ellisland on 3rd February 1789, that *"… I have been turning my lyre on the banks of the Nith. Some larger poetic plans that are floating in my imagination, or partly put in execution, I shall impart to you when I have the pleasure of meeting with you …"*. On the blank front and end pages Burns had added 12 new poems and writings.

The *Geddes Burns,* as it became known, spent some years at the Scots College in Valladolid in Spain where Geddes was rector, before returning with him to Scotland. Suffering from severe rheumatism, Geddes retired to Aberdeen in 1793.

Upon his death, the book travelled via his sister (although she was perhaps a niece) to London, and then to America, being bought by James Black in 1863. Black, an emigrant from Nairn who settled in Detroit, produced the book at the first meeting of the Burns Club of Detroit in 1867. Eventually the *Geddes Burns* found its way into the hands of American collector, WK Bixby, who had it photographed in 1908 as a limited edition. It is now in The Huntington Library, California.

Bishop John Geddes died in Aberdeen on 11th February 1799, aged 64.

The Episcopal Chapel (St Patrick's Church)
Cowgate, EH1 1TQ

Below: St Patrick's Church c1774 and in the present (bottom)

For 150 years, this church has been known as St Patrick's RC church.

Now St Patrick's RC Church, this is where Burns' collaborator on the *Scots Musical Museum*, Stephen Clarke, played the organ.

The building was originally built in the mid-1700s by the Episcopalians. They named the church St Paul's because it was to the writings of St Paul that many reformers turned for their religious inspiration. In the mid-1800s, the Episcopalians sold the building to the Church of Scotland and moved into the much larger St Mary's Cathedral near Haymarket.

By the middle of the 19th century, the Irish population of the Cowgate was increasing. The Church of Scotland sold the building to the Roman Catholic Church to accommodate this new group of worshippers and the name was changed to St Patrick's after the patron saint of Ireland.

Stephen Clarke worked on harmonising the melodies of the old Scots airs. When Burns first met him in 1787, Clarke was the organist at St Paul's. Clarke's son took the job as organist when he died in 1797.

The church's design has been changed over the years; the congregation now normally enters by a door on the west side.

Opposite this door on the walls of a side altar, are 4 paintings which, along with a painting on the ceiling, are the only surviving Alexander Runciman murals after a severe fire in Penicuik House destroyed all other examples of this work.

St Patrick's RC Church
40 High Street,
Old Town,
Edinburgh
EH1 1TQ
0131 556 1973
www.stpatricksparish.co.uk
office@stpatricksparish.co.uk
Wheelchair access is provided through the side door in South Gray's Close.

Reverend Archibald Alison

1757–1839 Writer

Cowgate

Reverend Archibald Alison had an excellent reputation as a clergyman and writer, and socialised in the highest literary circles in Edinburgh. After spending some years in England, Alison became a senior minister at the Episcopal Chapel, Cowgate, a position he held until his retirement in 1831.

When he lived in England, Alison became a friend of the engineer Thomas Telford, who also wrote poetry throughout his life. Telford sent a copy of his first published poem to Robert Burns in 1779, when he (Telford) was 22 years old.

Alison, a writer himself, met Robert Burns in February 1789 and the following year sent Burns a copy of his book, *Essays on the Nature and Principles of Taste* to which Burns replied enthusiastically.

Above: Archibald Alison

Below: Burns' correspondence with Alison

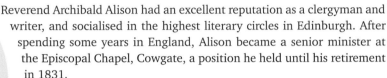

ELLISLAND, NEAR DUMFRIES,
14th February, 1791.

SIR,

You must by this time have set me down as one of the most ungrateful of men. You did me the honour to present me with a book, which does honour to science and the intellectual powers of man, and I have not even so much as acknowledged the receipt of it. The fact is, you yourself are to blame for it. Flattered as I was by your telling me that you wished to have my opinion of the work, the old spiritual enemy of mankind, who knows well that vanity is one of the sins that most easily beset me, put it into my head to ponder over the performance with the look-out of a critic, and to draw up, forsooth, a deep-learned, digest of strictures on a composition of which, in fact, until I read the book, I did not even know the first principles. I own, Sir, that, at first glance, several of your propositions startled me as paradoxical. That the martial clangor of a trumpet had something in it vastly more grand, heroic, and sublime, than the twingle-twangle of a Jew's harp; that the delicate flexure of a rose-twig, when the half-blown flower is heavy with the tears of the dawn, was infinitely more beautiful and elegant than the upright stub of a burdock, and that from something innate and independent of all associations of ideas—these I had set down as irrefragable, orthodox truths, until perusing your book shook my faith. In short, Sir, except Euclid's Elements of Geometry, which I made a shift to unravel by my father's fireside in the winter evenings of the first season I' held the plough, I never read a book which gave me such a quantum of information, and added so much to my stock of ideas as your "Essay on the Principles of Taste." One thing, Sir, you must forgive my mentioning as an uncommon merit in the work—I mean the language. To clothe abstract philosophy in elegance of style, sounds something like a contradiction in terms; but you have convinced me that they are quite compatible.

I enclose you some poetic bagatelles of my late composition. The one in print is my first essay in the way of telling a tale. I am, Sir, &c.,

R. B.

St Cecilia's Hall (Museum of Instruments)

Cowgate, EH1 1NQ

Below: St Cecilia's Hall
Bottom: Robert Burns by Peter Taylor

Saint Cecilia's Hall is named after the patron saint of musicians, St Cecilia. It is now not only a famous auditorium, dating from 1763, and the oldest concert hall in Scotland, but is also a world famous museum and research centre. It houses about 50 of the most important early keyboard instruments in the world. It also has a Burns connection.

Burns seems to have attended at least one concert in the auditorium here and because of this association, the Hall has on loan from the SNPG the smaller of the two Peter Taylor portraits (approx 9×8-in). Burns sat on three occasions for this unjustly neglected portrait.

The existence of this work only came to light in 1812 and it could be seen on the first floor of the Hall (item number 22) opposite the door to the exhibition.

Also of interest to Burns followers is an excellent portrait of George Thomson which is located on the left-side wall of the auditorium. George Thomson engaged Burns to work on the *Select Collection of Scottish Airs* and another portrait of him can be seen in the Writers' Museum. Thomson was a violinist of some note and played in this very auditorium.

St Cecilia's Hall
Cowgate
Edinburgh
EH1 1NQ
www.music.ed.ac.uk/euchmi/sch

Above: St Cecilia's Hall

At the time of writing, St Cecilia's Hall is closed for major redevelopment with plans to re-open in September 2016. For further information on the project see www.stcecilias.ed.ac.uk

Girolamo Stabilini
c1762–1815 Violinist and conductor

Girolamo, also known as Hieronymo, Stabilini was born in Rome in 1762 and his reputation as a young and promising musician led to his being invited to take leadership at St Cecilia's Hall concerts in 1783.

He started his almost weekly concerts in 1784, leading the orchestra, playing solo and accompanying singers such as Domenico Corri with whom he became very friendly. Stabilini soon became a favourite with audiences and public, using many Scots tunes in his concerts.

Stabilini was a Freemason and it is likely that Burns would have met him at one of the meetings in St John Street. Burns commented on Stabilini's concerts on several occasions in his letters and it has to be assumed that he attended the St Cecilia's Concerts more than once.

Above: Girolamo Stabilini

In 1794 Stabilini went to London to take part in the Handelian Concerts in Westminister Abbey. He also regularly played at Gordon Castle and Huntly Lodge.

Stabilini stayed at several addresses in Edinburgh. In 1787 he lived at No. 6 Shakespeare Square, the site of the Theatre Royal, opposite Register House. By 1790 he moved to the North Side of St James Square, and in 1796 he moved again, this time to North St James Street.

It was said that he injured his bow arm in an incident at Leith races and never played quite so well again. According to David Johnstone's *Music and Society in Lowland Scotland,* Stabilini would have gone on to greater things had he not turned to drink. Another report suggests that he was broken down by dissipation.

Girolamo Stabilini died of dropsy at his later address of Rose Street, Edinburgh on 13th July 1815, aged 53, and is buried in St Cuthbert's Graveyard.

His tombstone is built into the old wall on the right of the path leading from the main, or west, entrance.

Domenico Corri
1746–1825 Composer and conductor

Corri was an Italian composer, conductor and music publisher. Also born in Rome, he and his wife, a singer, were invited to Edinburgh in 1771 by Dr Burney. Corri became conductor of the Musical Society, a position he retained for 18 years. George Thomson said it was Corri's singing of old Scots songs that led him to begin a collection of them.

Prior to travelling to Edinburgh, Corri lived for two years at the house of the exiled Charles Edward Stuart (Bonnie Prince Charlie) in Rome. Charles was an amateur cellist and would often be accompanied by Corri.

Above: Domenico Corri and Mrs Alice Corri

Johann Georg Christoph Schetky
1737–1824 Musician

Cowgate

Johann Georg Christoph Schetky was born in Darmstadt, Hesse (now Germany), on 19th August 1737.

Schetky was a member of the Darmstadt Court Ochestra until 1768. After playing his own works throughout the Austro-Hungarian Empire, and France, he played in London in 1772. While in London he secured the position of principal cellist to the Edinburgh Music Society at the St Cecilia's Hall concerts in Edinburgh which were of great repute.

One music critic said his Cello Sonata opus 4, number 4 (1776) *"was surpassed only by Beethoven himself"*.

He married in Edinburgh and his accomplished taste and good manners secured invitations from the highest in society, as well as mixing with the most distinguished literary characters of the time.

Schetky was also a member of Lodge Canongate Kilwinning No. 2 and it is likely that Burns would have met him at one of the meetings or clubs in the city. They certainly met and worked together, Burns writing in a letter of 24th January 1788 to Agnes that he had been drinking with Mr Schetky, and that *"he had set the song finely"*. The song was *Clarinda, Mistress of my Soul*.

Below: Johann Georg Christoph Schetky

His son, born in Edinburgh on 11th August 1778, was given the more anglicised version of his father's name, John George Christopher Schetky, trained with the artist Alexander Nasmyth and became a renowned painter of naval scenes. He died in London on 28th January 1874 in his 96th year. He is buried in Paddington Cemetery.

Johann Schetky died in Edinburgh on 30th November 1824, aged 84, and is buried in an unmarked grave in Canongate Graveyard.

His grave is described as being, *"West Side. Six feet north of Sharp's Ground and four feet south west of Langley's stone."*

Clarinda (Mistress of my soul)

Clarinda, mistress of my soul,
The measur'd time is run!
The wretch beneath the dreary pole,
So marks his latest sun.

To what dark cave of frozen night
Shall poor Sylvander hie;
Depriv'd of thee, his life and light,
The Sun of all his joy.

We part – but by these precious drops,
That fill thy lovely eyes!
No other light shall guide my steps,
Till thy bright beams arise.

She, the fair Sun of all her sex,
Has blest my glorious day:
And shall a glimmering Planet fix
My worship to its ray?

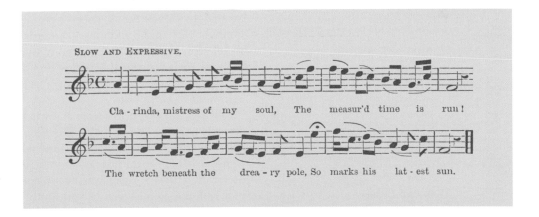

SLOW AND EXPRESSIVE.

Cla - rinda, mistress of my   soul,   The   measur'd time   is   run !

The wretch beneath the   drea - ry pole, So   marks his   lat - est sun.

Peter Taylor

1757–88 Artist

Cowgate

Peter Taylor was the first to paint Robert Burns and one of only three artists who Burns actually sat for.

Peter Taylor was a house and coach painter. He met Robert Burns at a dinner in December 1786, enjoying each other's company so much that Burns was invited to breakfast the following morning. Burns duly arrived at the Taylor house in Edinburgh and, after breakfast, the portrait was started.

Below: Flyer for the sale of Taylor prints

Burns returned over three days, sitting for one hour on the first two days and for several hours on the third, before other business intervened.

The existence of the painting was not discovered until 1812. Peter Taylor died in Marseille on 20th December 1788, aged 31, only 2 years after carrying out the work, and this may be one reason why the paintings never came to public view for so many years.

Taylor painted two portraits from that sitting. The original was held by Taylor's wife after his death and she hid it away in the upper leaf of a clothes' press, refusing to show it to anyone for many years. It is the smaller of the two at 8½ × 8-in.

James Hogg tells how he was invited to a meeting by Gilbert Burns, Robert's brother, and found Robert Ainslie and others discussing how to get sight of the original portrait of Burns. At this time Hogg was sure that it must be a hoax as he thought it unlikely that such a portrait could be concealed for so long.

However, they tried to obtain an invitation to see the painting through Miss Dudgeon, who was a relative of Miss Taylor and lived with the widow in her flat on the first floor in West Register Street. At first Mrs Taylor was not co-operative but, with the promise that Gilbert Burns would attend, she finally relented and allowed them to visit her flat. Although she allowed each of those present to look at the portrait for as long as they wished, Mrs Taylor never allowed the painting to leave her hand at any time. According to those present who had known Burns it was obvious that this was a very good likeness.

Sales of prints were advertised in January 1830 with testimonials to the remarkable likeness from Sir Walter Scott, Gilbert Burns, James Hogg, Jean Burns, Peter Hill, Miss Dunlop, Agnes McLehose and others.

The smaller portrait was bequeathed to the Scottish National Portrait Gallery by the Taylor family in 1927 and at the time of writing is on loan to St Cecilia's Hall, while the larger portrait, painted on board, hangs in the Writers' Museum. It is attributed to Taylor and remarkably, its existence only came to light in 1893.

No other work from Peter Taylor has ever been found, which may cast doubt on his ability as a portrait painter, something he had in common with Alexander Nasmyth.

It is interesting to note that the oldest surviving outdoor statue of Robert Burns is in the town of Camperdown in Victoria, Australia, and is based on the Taylor portrait. The sculptor was John Greenshields whose studio was in Broomhill, Glasgow. Peter Taylor's son William became one of the early settlers in Victoria and he had the statue shipped to him, subsequently presenting it to the town in 1883. In 2009 having been badly vandalised, it was put into storage while an effort was made to raise funds for the restoration. Happily, Aus $85,000 was raised to complete the restoration, including shipping out stone from Drumhead Quarry in Scotland, and the restored statue was unveiled in 2012 by Victoria's Premier.

Above: The restored statue of Burns in its new, indoor location at the Camperdown Civic Centre, Victoria.

High Street

1 Carruber's Close

2 Bell's Wynd

3 Anchor Close

4 Craig's Close (site of)

5 St Giles' and the site of the Luckenbooths

6 Parliament Square

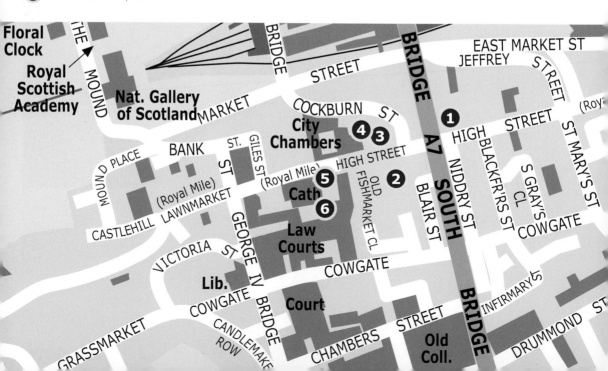

Carrubber's Close
135 High Street, EH1 1SJ

Top: Carruber's [sic] Close
Plaque
Middle: Carrubber's Close today
Bottom: Carrubber's Close in
Burns' day

Burns knew at least three people who lived here and would have been a frequent visitor.

Carrubber's Close dates from before 1531 and after 1688 was nicknamed the last stronghold of faithful Jacobites.

This close was the home of Samuel Mitchelson, the employer of Robert Ainslie who accompanied Burns on the first part of his tour of the Borders in May 1787.

Burns first met Ainslie in 1787. They both shared a love of socialising. Burns said of him: *"I have not a friend upon earth besides yourself, to whom I can talk nonsense without forfeiting some degree of his esteem."*

Burns later trusted Ainslie with knowledge of his relationships with Agnes McLehose and May Cameron. Ainslie became friendly with Agnes, wrote to her about Burns and also regularly visited her when she stayed in General's Entry.

Burns was a frequent guest of Mitchelson and also his close friend, Sir William Forbes of Pitsligo who lived here before moving to the New Town.

At the head of the close lived Captain Matthew Henderson, war hero and member of the Crochallan Fencibles. When he died in 1789 Burns wrote a powerful elegy to him, and in a note to the poem added, *"I loved the man much and have not flattered his memory."*

Allan Ramsay Snr. constructed a theatre here in 1737 and there is a plaque commemorating it at the close entrance. The theatre was an expensive, but short-lived, scheme when it was closed shortly after opening by city magistrates when the Church opposed the granting of a licence. The theatre then went through many guises, such as a debating and lecture chamber, and ironically, several and various religious uses over the years including as a Catholic schoolroom before being demolished to make way for Jeffrey Street.

Craig's Close
29 Cockburn Street, EH1 1BN

Burns studied French here under Louis Cauvin. Edinburgh publisher, William Creech, had a house here.

Situated off 265 High Street, the top section, or head of the close, was removed with the expansion of the City Chambers in 1930–34. The northern section remains, descending from Cockburn Street to Market Street.

The Isle of Man Arms in Craig's Close, kept by James Mann, was the meeting place for the Cape Club. Members were given humorous names with character traits that they had to use on subsequent meetings. They adorned themselves with various forms of royal regalia, badges and insignia which denoted their Cape Club rank. Intricately engraved maces made from long pokers, and adorned with mottos, formed the sword and sceptre of the king.

The Cape Club was well known for the 'high jinks' its members got up to during a meeting and included in its famous membership were Robert Fergusson, Alexander Runciman, Sir Henry Raeburn and the infamous Deacon Brodie.

Provincial Cape Clubs were set up in Glasgow, Manchester, London and an apparently successful branch in Charleston, South Carolina.

Cauvin had a house at the head of the close, near the High Street and it was here that he gave Burns and Beugo French lessons. The lessons were at 9 o'clock in the evening as Burns was generally working during the daytime, checking proofs.

William Creech

1745–1815 Publisher

Craig's Close

William Creech, the son of a minister, was born in Newbattle, Midlothian in 1745. His father died, leaving his mother to bring him up first in Dalkeith and later, Perth.

After he began medical studies at Edinburgh University he was found a position with a printing and publishing business whose owner, Alexander Kincaid, knew his mother.

He travelled throughout Europe with his boyhood friend, Lord Kilmaurs, who was later to become the 14th Earl of Glencairn and Burns' patron.

Creech entered into a partnership with Alexander Kincaid in 1771, Kincaid retiring in 1772. Creech then ran his publishing business, centred in the Luckenbooths for the next 44 years until he died.

His Luckenbooth shop was famous, frequented by writers, the gentry, and many businessmen. For over 40 years it was the centre of the world of literature; Burns, works by Adam Smith, Dugald Stewart, Henry MacKenzie, Blair, Beattie and many others were published by Creech. Work was sent from London to be published by Creech. The land around the shop came to be known as Creech's Land and the 'breakfast room' as Creech's Levee as so many writers wanted to visit just to spend time there mingling with the literati of the day.

In 1788 Creech was a member of the jury in the trial of the infamous Deacon Brodie. Within days, his account of the trial and execution was for sale in his High Street bookshop.

Brodie was a town councillor and an apparently upright and trustworthy citizen. A member of the Cape Club, he socialised with the Edinburgh gentry and was the city's most respected and trustworthy locksmith, but he used his knowledge to make extra keys which he used to rob the richest members of Edinburgh society.

Creech had been a town councillor from 1780 and, through his involvement with the Edinburgh Council and his attendance

Above: William Creech

Below: Creech's Land, in the Luckenbooths

at various social gatherings in the city, it is unlikely that Creech did not know Brodie.

Lord Glencairn asked Creech to undertake the publication of an Edinburgh edition of Burns' poems and Creech agreed, advising a subscription for which he promised to subscribe for 500 copies. Creech tried to get Cadell's of London to take some of the edition of 3,000 but on the 23rd April agreed to guarantee the entire publication himself. Later, on the advice of Henry MacKenzie, Burns sold his copyright for 100 guineas.

Creech, being notoriously mean, delayed payment of all sums to Burns, causing Burns to stay in Edinburgh for much longer than intended as he waited for Creech to settle up with him.

Burns wrote to Creech in exasperation at the delay and Creech did settle eventually, paying him all sums due and Burns apparently forgave him by collaborating with him on the two-volume edition of November 1793. In a letter to Lord Glencairn, Burns writes that he hoped for £200; he must have been a happy man when he was paid between £500 and £600.

When Burns delayed in correcting proofs, Creech went ahead with publication anyway.

Creech wrote many articles on Edinburgh and the huge social and housing problems caused by the high population and development work round the city. He was genuinely concerned for the wellbeing of Edinburgh's citizens.

William Creech died, unmarried, in Edinburgh on 14th January 1815 at the age of 70, and is buried in Greyfriars Kirkyard.

His portrait by Sir Henry Raeburn hangs in the Scottish National Portrait Gallery.

Right: Burns' letter to Glencairn

TO THE EARL OF GLENCAIRN.

EDINBURGH, 1788.

I KNOW your Lordship will disapprove of my ideas in a request I am going to make to you; but I have weighed, long and seriously weighed, my situation, my hopes, and turn of mind, and am fully fixed to my scheme if I can possibly effectuate it. I wish to get into the Excise: I am told that your Lordship's interest will easily procure me the grant from the Commissioners; and your Lordship's patronage and goodness, which have already rescued me from obscurity, wretchedness, and exile, embolden me to ask that interest. You have like-wise put it in my power to save the little tie of home that sheltered an aged mother, two brothers, and three sisters from destruction. There, my Lord, you have bound me over to the highest gratitude.

My brother's farm is but a wretched lease, but I think he will probably weather out the remaining seven years of it; and after the assistance which I have given and will give him, to keep the family together, I think, by my guess, I shall have rather better than two hundred pounds; and instead of seeking, what is almost impossible at present to find, a farm that I can certainly live by, with so small a stock, I shall lodge this sum in a banking-house, a sacred deposit, excepting only the calls of uncommon distress or necessitous old age. . . . .

R. B.

Lament For The Absence Of William Creech, Publisher

Auld chuckie Reekie's sair distrest,
Down droops her ance weel burnish'd crest,
Nae joy her bonie buskit nest
Can yield ava,
Her darling bird that she lo'es best –
Willie's awa!

O Willie was a witty wight,
And had o' things an unco' sleight,
Auld Reekie aye he keepit tight,
And trig an' braw:
But now they'll busk her like a fright, –
Willie's awa!

The stiffest o' them a' he bow'd,
The bauldest o' them a' he cow'd;
They durst nae mair than he allow'd,
That was a law:
We've lost a birkie weel worth gowd;
Willie's awa!

Now gawkies, tawpies, gowks and fools,
Frae colleges and boarding schools,
May sprout like simmer puddock-stools
In glen or shaw;
He wha could brush them down to mools –
Willie's awa!

The brethren o' the Commerce-chaumer
May mourn their loss wi' doolfu' clamour;
He was a dictionar and grammar
Among them a';
I fear they'll now mak mony a stammer;
Willie's awa!

Nae mair we see his levee door
Philosophers and poets pour,
And toothy critics by the score,
In bloody raw!
The adjutant o' a' the core –
Willie's awa!

Now worthy Gregory's Latin face,
Tytler's and Greenfield's modest grace;
Mackenzie, Stewart, such a brace
As Rome ne'er saw;
They a' maun meet some ither place,
Willie's awa!

Poor Burns ev'n Scotch Drink canna quicken,
He cheeps like some bewilder'd chicken
Scar'd frae it's minnie and the cleckin,
By hoodie-craw;
Grieg's gien his heart an unco kickin,
Willie's awa!

Now ev'ry sour-mou'd girnin blellum,
And Calvin's folk, are fit to fell him;
Ilk self-conceited critic skellum
His quill may draw;
He wha could brawlie ward their bellum
Willie's awa!

Up wimpling stately Tweed I've sped,
And Eden scenes on crystal Jed,
And Ettrick banks, now roaring red,
While tempests blaw;
But every joy and pleasure's fled,
Willie's awa!

May I be Slander's common speech;
A text for Infamy to preach;
And lastly, streekit out to bleach
In winter snaw;
When I forget thee, Willie Creech,
Tho' far awa!

May never wicked Fortune touzle him!
May never wicked men bamboozle him!
Until a pow as auld's Methusalem
He canty claw!
Then to the blessed new Jerusalem,
Fleet wing awa!

Henry Mackenzie
1745–1831 Writer
Craig's Close

Henry Mackenzie was a Scottish novelist who was born in Edinburgh in August 1745 and educated at the Royal High School and Edinburgh University.

When, after 7 years, he had failed to interest publishers in his first book, *The Man of Feeling*, he self-published it in 1771 and it was an immediate success.

In 1776 he married Penuel, daughter of Sir Ludovic Grant of Grant with whom he would have 11 children.

In Edinburgh he belonged to a literary club which established a weekly periodical called *The Mirror*, which ran from January 1779 to May 1780. Mackenzie was the editor and chief contributor.

The *Mirror* was followed by *The Lounger*, which ran for nearly 2 years and had the distinction of publishing the earliest tributes to the genius that was Robert Burns, written by Mackenzie on the 9th December 1786. It was he who created the myth of the *'ploughman poet',* which Burns played up to.

Mackenzie admired Burns' work enormously, recommending him to his literary friends. When Burns was to embark on his highland tour with Nicol in 1787, Mackenzie gave Burns a letter of introduction to his brother-in-law, Sir James Grant.

A Tory, he anonymously wrote many articles intended to counteract the French Revolution. When he defended the policies of William Pitt, his loyalty was rewarded with the office of Controller of Taxes for Scotland in 1804.

Below: Henry Mackenzie

Mackenzie wrote *A Life of Doctor Blacklock* which was prefixed to the 1793 edition of the poet's work, and had a considerable influence on Sir Walter Scott, who dedicated his *Waverley* novels to Mackenzie.

An active sportsman in his old age, he lived at No. 6 Heriot Row in Edinburgh in his later years.

Henry MacKenzie died on 14th January 1831 aged 86 and is buried in Greyfriars Kirkyard.

A bust of MacKenzie can be seen in the Scottish National Portrait Gallery. A portrait of Mackenzie by Sir Henry Raeburn is in the National Portrait Gallery, London.

Louis Cauvin
1754–1825 Teacher
Craig's Close

Above: Louis Cauvin

Louis Cauvin (sometimes known as Lewis Cavine) was born in the village of Jock's Lodge, Edinburgh in 1745. According to some accounts his father, also Louis, was a French Huguenot officer who fled the country to avoid the consequences of a fatal duel in which he was involved.

There is an equally exciting version that gripped not only Edinburgh but the whole of the United Kingdom and France. It was that he came to Edinburgh to bear witness in a trial known as the 'Douglas Cause' having served as a footman in the family of Lady Jane Douglas during her stay in Paris. This was a hugely controversial case that lasted many years from 1748 to 1767. It led to lawyers duelling, and was deliberated upon in the House of Lords, eventually requiring soldiers on the streets to restore order.

Cauvin became a tenant of a small farm at Jock's Lodge, near Restalrig, a village in a suburb of Edinburgh. He taught French language lessons until his death in 1778, leaving a family of 3 sons and 3 daughters.

As the young Louis had assisted his father in his French classes, he continued teaching the French language. He was educated in the High School and College then studied for 2 years at the University of Paris before returning to his school in Edinburgh.

His school rooms were in the north side of the High Street, immediately in front of the Old Guard House, which was very near to the Tron Church.

He was apparently very strict, demanding punctuality and hard work from his pupils and abhorred injustice and oppression. Despite his reputation as a stern taskmaster, he brought orphans into his employment, an indication of the charitable work he was to continue in later life.

He was a very good friend of Robert Burns who approached him to learn the French language. Burns had been in conversation with a French woman and was dismayed to find that she had difficulty in understanding his French. Although Burns still read books in French it had been many years since John Murdoch had taught him, and knowing of Cauvin's reputation as the best teacher of the French language in the city he went to Cauvin to re-learn the language.

As Burns worked during the day proof-reading the *Edinburgh Edition*, the only time that suited both men was at 9pm and Cauvin agreed to become his tutor. Burns and his friend, the engraver John Beugo, attended classes 3 times a week for 3 months.

Cauvin later said of Burns, "*he made more progress in the acquisition of the language in these three months, than any ordinary pupil could have done in as many years.*"

Like his father, Cauvin rented a large farm in the Duddingston area to the south-east of Arthur's Seat. He worked there for over 20 years and he lived there in the summer months. In the winter he remained in town; in 1786–88 his address is listed in *Williamson's Directory* as Bishop's Land, before moving some time later to the head of Craig's Close, off the High Street. It is likely that this is where Burns and Beugo attended classes.

While the bottom section of Craig's Close still exists from Cockburn Street to Market Street, the top section of the close at the High Street, where Cauvin lived, was demolished with the extension of the City Chambers.

Acquiring much wealth from his very successful school, he built the house of Louisfield, opposite the farm on the road to Jock's Lodge. This house was to become Cauvin's Hospital. Before his death he bequeathed it to provide for the maintenance and education of 20 boys for a period of 6 years, who were of the same class as himself, namely the sons of teachers and farmers, and between the ages of 6 and 8. The hospital opened in 1833 and was administered by trustees. The trustees stated that the object of the school was to lay the foundation for a professional education for schoolmasters, so that as many of the boys, as circumstances allowed, became skilful and accomplished teachers.

The building still stands on Willowbrae Road, near Duddingston, now being used as housing for the elderly.

Above: Cauvin's Hospital

When the area of Duddingston was laid out and plots put up for sale, the very wealthy Cauvin, Colonel Graham and a Mr Scott bought up many of the plots between them.

Cauvin purchased a small strip of ground lying between the mansion house of Colonel Graham and the main street of the village and proceeded to build a house on it, first declining an offer from the colonel to buy the land.

However as the windows of the house overlooked the colonel's grounds, the colonel raised the garden wall to block this view.

Cauvin then had the roof taken down and added a further two stories forcing the colonel to raise the wall a corresponding proportion.

This 'game' was brought to a halt by the death of Cauvin.

The Tower, as it was known, was nicknamed 'Cauvin's Folly', and the land on which it was built was bought by the colonel's son sometime later.

The tower was demolished in 1895.

Louis Cauvin died aged 71, on 24th December 1825 and is buried in the family tomb in the burial ground in the village of Restalrig.

His instructions were that his corpse was to be watched for a proper time, the door to be taken off and the space be built up with ashlar stone, shut for ever and never be opened.

James Johnson
1753–1811 Printer, engraver and music seller
Bell's Wynd, EH1 1QY

Burns edited and composed many songs for James Johnson's *The Scots Musical Museum*. The volumes were printed here.

James Johnson was baptised on 6th May 1753 at Shorthope, Ettrick in Selkirkshire, the son of a herdsman. Despite these humble beginnings Johnson successfully completed his training as an engraver.

James Johnson had a shop in Bell's Wynd. When he invented a printing process for reproducing sheet music on etched pewter plates, he decided to make a collection of Scots songs, called *The Scots Musical Museum*, to sell through his music shop in the Lawnmarket.

When he met Burns, the first volume of 100 songs was already in the press and Burns contributed only 4 songs to this edition. Burns was enthusiastic about the idea and when Johnson invited Burns to collaborate, Burns' enthusiasm took over the project and he contributed over 200 of his own compositions, rewriting and restructuring many others. Burns refused any fee for any of the work he did for Johnson.

Above: James Johnson

Three further volumes were published during Burns' lifetime with a fifth ready to go to press when he died. It took Johnson another 7 years to produce the final sixth volume, which consisted mainly of Burns' work. *The Scots Musical Museum* has remained the most important collection of Scots songs to the present day. As well as many works by Burns the *Museum* contains songs by Agnes McLehose (*Talk Not of Love, To a Blackbird Singing in a Tree*) and Dr Blacklock.

Dr Blacklock contributed 10 or so pieces to the *Museum* and wrote the music for 4: *My Love Has Forsaken Me, Ye River So Limpid and Dear, Forbear Gentle Youth, When Dear Evanthe.*

Burns made only minor alterations to Agnes' songs, but was less keen on Dr Blacklock's talent: *"I have still a good number of Dr Blacklock's Songs among my hands, but they take sad hacking and hewing."*

The musical editor was Stephen Clark, who was musical Director of the Episcopal Chapel in the Cowgate. When he died his son took his place as musical editor.

Johnson eventually moved his shop to the Luckenbooths but his printing process was eclipsed with the invention in 1795 of lithography by Alois Senefelder. Despite the popularity of the *Museum,* Johnson remained poor.

James Johnson died in poverty at home in the Lawnmarket on 26th February 1811. His widow, left destitute, was the subject of a public appeal in March 1819, but died very shortly after the appeal commenced.

Ye Jacobites By Name

Ye Jacobites by name, give an ear, give an ear,
Ye Jacobites by name, give an ear,
Ye Jacobites by name,
Your fautes I will proclaim,
Your doctrines I maun blame, you shall hear.

What is Right and what is Wrang, by the law, by the law?
What is Right and what is Wrang by the law?
What is Right, and what is Wrang?
A short sword, and a lang,
A weak arm and a strang, for to draw.

What makes heroic strife, famed afar, famed afar?
What makes heroic strife famed afar?
What makes heroic strife?
To whet th' assassin's knife,
Or hunt a Parent's life, wi' bluidy war?

Then let your schemes alone, in the state, in the state,
Then let your schemes alone in the state.
Then let your schemes alone,
Adore the rising sun,
And leave a man undone, to his fate.

Anchor Close
243 High Street, EH1 1XD

This is where the *Edinburgh Edition* of the poems of Robert Burns was printed. Burns sat here frequently, correcting the proofs. Burns also frequented a tavern in this close.

When Robert Burns came to Edinburgh in November 1786, Creech, the publisher of the *Edinburgh Edition*, took Burns to William Smellie's printing works, situated at the foot of Anchor Close where the printing would take place.

Below: Anchor Close plaque

Robert Burns would attend almost every day, not only to correct proofs but also to converse with the owner who was very knowledgeable in a wide variety of subjects and an acknowledged expert in many. In 1771 Smellie became editor and compiler of the newly created *Encyclopaedia Britannica*.

Printing in 1786 was a time-consuming process. Each page, which would be the exact size of the finished article, had to be 'set'. Individual letters, made from lead, were assembled together on a wooden block to make a replica of the page. The letters were assembled in reverse before being put into the press, and each sheet was printed individually, and manually. The initial sheets would be called the proof and it was these that Burns would check for mistakes.

Below: Anchor Close

Burns frequented Smellie's premises so often that he had his own stool, and if someone else happened to sit upon it, the mere mention that the stool was Burns' was enough to leave it vacant once more. The stool can be seen in the Writers' Museum.

The first *Edinburgh Edition* sold out and a second *Edinburgh Edition* had to be printed immediately. As it was so expensive to have each letter manufactured, pages previously assembled couldn't be kept and the typesetting process had to be repeated, with each page having to be proof-read again. After the first batch had been printed, the type had to be re-set. An error crept into a line in the *Address to a Haggis*, where by "*Auld Scotland wants nae skinking ware*", became "*Auld Scotland wants nae stinking ware*". The second form of the 1787 edition has thus become known as the *Stinking Burns.*

At the head of Anchor Close there was a famous tavern, Dawney Douglas's, kept by Daniel Douglas, who came from the Highlands. It is said that on one occasion Queen Mary slept here, but in 1786 it was frequented by lawyers and businessmen.

Smellie, who was known as a lover of 'recreation' and convivial company, was a very regular attendee at Dawney Douglas's. He was a founder member of a club here called the Crochallan Fencibles.

Above: Walter Scott's father

Right, inset: Anchor Close

The name Crochallan was partly derived from a Gaelic song *Chrodh Chailein* and Fencibles so as to identify with the Fencible regiments that were being raised for the defence of the country. All members of the Crochallan Fencibles were given some mock military rank, major, colonel etc. Smellie was the hangman and it was his duty to drill new recruits.

All new members had to undergo a test of 'social fitness'. This was the equivalent of today's 'roasts' where a celebrity is abused in a way that would show respect by his abusers. When Burns was introduced in January 1787, Smellie and the others carried out the ordeal in a vigorous way and Smellie found Burns fully able to cope with all that was thrown at him, and it became a regular form of amusement to pit Burns against the Hangman. The Crochallan Fencibles Club exists to this day.

Sir Walter Scott's parents lived in Anchor Close until 1771.

Andrew Bell

1726–1809 Engraver

Anchor Close

Andrew Bell was born in Edinburgh in 1726.

His first work was engraving names on gentlemen's plates, dog collars and the like. In 1781 he engraved all the plates in Smellie's translation of Buffon's *Natural History*.

One of his customers was the Scottish Society of Freemasons and from 1755, he himself belonged to Lodge St David Edinburgh No. 36.

Bell was the proprietor of the *Encyclopaedia Britannica* along with Colin MacFarquhar. When MacFarquhar died in 1793 the book became the complete property of Bell. This made Bell a very rich man. The third edition of 10,000 copies realised the sum of £42,000.

Bell was a colourful character, as was his friend Smellie, his editor and compiler of the first edition. He was small, with crooked legs and an enormous nose. He would sometimes substitute a *papier-mâché* nose to the amusement of onlookers.

Andrew Bell regularly took exercise on horseback. His horse was very tall and at 4 feet 6 inches, Bell was not, forcing him to use a small ladder to mount it. He was sufficiently good humoured to laugh at himself.

Above: Andrew Bell

He produced almost all of the copperplate engravings in the first 4 editions of *Britannica*, and for the first edition produced 3 full pages of anatomically correct depictions of dissected female pelvises and foetuses in the womb for the midwifery article. These illustrations shocked King George III so much that he commanded that the offending pages be ripped from every copy.

Andrew Bell died in Edinburgh in 1809.

After his death, the encyclopaedia was bought from the executors by his son-in-law, Thomas Bonnar, who carried on the printing at the Grove, Fountainbridge. Bell had previously had an argument with Bonnar and had refused to speak to him for the last 10 years of his life.

The *Encyclopaedia Britannica* is still produced, now available in a digital version.

William Smellie

1740–95 Editor, writer and printer

Anchor Close

William Smellie was born in the Pleasance, a suburb of Edinburgh. He first went to the parish school at Duddingston before going to the High School at the age of 10.

On 1st October 1752 he was apprenticed to a printer and, with the permission of the employers, attended classes at the university.

In 1757, aged 17, he won the silver medal from the Philosophical Society for the most accurate edition of a Latin classic, *Terence,* which he set-up and edited.

Right inset: William Smellie and Andrew Bell by John Kay

In September 1759 he became an assistant editor of *The Scots Magazine* and also continued his university studies, completing courses in theology and medicine. To oversee the printing of a book on Hebrew grammar he attended a class on Oriental language. Then came a class on botany, and he produced in 1765 a dissertation which won the gold medal of Dr Hope, Professor of Botany at the University and was later printed in the *Encyclopaedia Britannica*. When Professor Hope took ill, he entrusted Smellie to tutor his classes while he was incapacitated.

With Smellie's well-known enjoyment of 'recreation' it is little wonder that Burns enjoyed his company. With 2 editions of his book to proof-read, and time spent in Dawney's Tavern with the Crochallan Fencibles, they would spend long days together.

Over the following years Smellie was to become interested in medical science and natural history, resulting in several ventures as both a writer and publisher.

When, in 1771 the *Encyclopaedia Britannica* was started he was employed as editor and compiler, composing the principal articles and revising others.

In 1773, with Gilbert Stuart, he founded *The Edinburgh Magazine and Revue* which ran until 1776. In 1781 he was made Superintendent of the Museum of Natural History, completing a translation of Buffon's *Natural History,* while in 1783 he prepared a plan to undertake a statistical account of Scottish Parishes.

In 1790 the publisher Charles Elliot paid Smellie 1,000 guineas for the

Below: William Smellie

copyright of his *Philosophy of Natural History*.

In 1584 there were 6 different printing presses in the city of Edinburgh, but the business of printing did not make any considerable progress until well after the Act of Union. In 1763 there were still only 6 printing offices in Edinburgh but by 1790 there were 21, and by 1822 there were 44 offices with 150 printing presses in total. It was said (reported in *Pigot's Guide* in the 1820s) *"that the works executed by them are probably not surpassed, in elegance or correctness, by any in Europe. Sixty years ago Edinburgh had made no great figure in the literary world; but, since that period, men of genius have been more handsomely rewarded here, than in any other country."*

Burns and Smellie are known to have corresponded, but with the exception of a letter from Dumfries on 2nd January 1792, the letters have been lost. Destroyed is probably a more accurate word as, with their history together at The Fencibles, the contents would almost certainly be either libellous or obscene, and most likely both!

Burns introduced Smellie to Mrs Riddell in this letter, and Smellie visited her and her husband. He became the printer of her work and kept up correspondence with her until his death. Smellie was presented with the Freedom of the Burgh at Dumfries in September 1792.

William Smellie died on 24th June 1795 in Edinburgh at the age of 65. He is buried in the southern section of Greyfriars Kirkyard.

His portrait is in the Scottish National Portrait Gallery.

On William Smellie

Shrewd Willie Smellie to Crochallan came:
The old cock'd hat, the brown surtout the same;
His grisly beard just bristling in its might
('Twas four long nights and days to shaving-night);
His umcomb'd hoary locks, wild-staring thatch'd
A head for thought profound and clear unmatch'd;
Yet, tho his caustic wit was biting rude,
His heart was warm, benevolent, and good.

St Giles' Cathedral
High Street, EH1 1RE

St Giles' was the centre of Edinburgh life for many years and in his time here Burns lived and worked around its precincts. The Robert Burns Memorial window was installed here in 1985.

St Giles' Cathedral, also known as the High Kirk of Edinburgh, is the Mother Church of Presbyterianism and contains the Chapel of the Order of the Thistle.

The Order of the Thistle is an order of chivalry in Scotland. The order consists of the sovereign and 16 knights and ladies; in addition there are further knights, members of British royal family or foreign monarchs.

In July 2012, Prince William was installed as a Knight of the Order of the Thistle; the ceremony was attended by Queen Elizabeth II, The Duke of Edinburgh, Prince Charles and the Princess Royal.

Below: St Giles' Cathedral

There are records of a parish church in Edinburgh dating back to 854, served by a vicar from England. It is possible that the first church on the site was in use for several centuries before it was formally dedicated on 6 October 1243. The parish church of Edinburgh was subsequently reconsecrated and named in honour of the patron saint of the town, St Giles, whose feast day is celebrated on 1st September.

St Giles was a 7th-century hermit who lived in France and became patron saint of both the town and church.

In 1559 John Knox, who led the Scottish Reformation, was elected minister of Edinburgh and in 1560 became minister of St Giles', a position he held until 1572.

The Reformation was a western european movement leading to national churches breaking their ties with Rome. Knox required that all signs of Catholicism be removed from churches, not only in Edinburgh but throughout Scotland. In St Giles' the walls were whitewashed, ornate and decorated windows replaced with plain glass; brass candlesticks and the decorated pulpit were sold or melted down. The Magdalen Chapel in the Cowgate has the only existing pre-Reformation stained-glass window in the city.

Below: Site of the grave of John Knox

The reformers divided the interior of the church, adding partitions and making other uses of the space. The church has been a police and fire station, a school and a coal store. The Scottish guillotine was housed here, and in one corner, there was a prison for 'harlots and whores'.

The General Assembly of the Church of Scotland and the Scottish Parliament also met here.

John Knox died on 24th November 1527 aged about 60 and was buried in the Old Kirkyard, now the car park to the south side of St Giles'. The spot, in parking space No. 23, is indicated by a small square of yellow tarmac.

On Sunday 23rd July 1637 there was a riot in the city sparked by the decision of Charles I in London to impose Anglican services and the Book of Common Prayer on the Church of Scotland. Legend has it that Jenny Geddes, a street-seller, responded to this affront on Scottish Presbyterianism by throwing her stool at the Dean calling out, *"Deil colic the wame o' ye!"* (May the Devil give you an upset stomach).

The tumult inside the church spread into the streets outside. Soon there was rioting all over the city, spreading to other cities within days. When Charles I refused to back down there was a real threat that civil war would break out. This led to the signing of a National Covenant in 1638. This covenant called for adherence to beliefs enshrined by parliament and the rejection of 'new' doctrines.

Robert Burns called the mare he bought in Edinburgh Jenny Geddes in her honour and immortalised her in poetry.

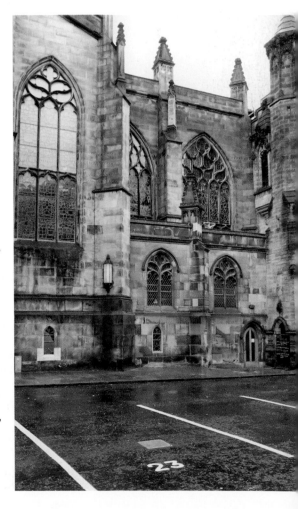

Right inset: The photo includes the Burns Window, stained glass window by Leifur Breidfjord, The New West Porch glass painting and metal screen artwork by Leifur Breidfjord and the *Baptismal Angel Kneeling,* by Danish Sculptor Bertel Thorvaldsen (1770–1844), originally modelled in Rome in 1827–1828

In Burns' time in Edinburgh, the church was in very poor condition and in need of much repair. It was very closed in by the Luckenbooths on the north side and the Tolbooth to the west and it was not until the early 1800s, when the Luckenbooths were removed, that renovation began.

William Burn, son of architect Robert Burn who designed Robert Fergusson's grave for Robert Burns, carried out a renovation in 1829. He removed the partitions, creating a single space, added new stained glass and covered the exterior walls with a smooth ashlar.

In 1977 another major renovation project began that lasted until 2008. This included major repairs to virtually all of the building. Among many other alterations and additions, the interior was lightened and a magnificent new organ was added.

In 1985 the Robert Burns Memorial Window, designed by Leifur Breidfjord, an Icelandic Master of Stained Glass and artist, was added to St Giles'.

This very large window, of a semi-abstract style, situated above the west door caused some controversy when installed and continues to do so. It celebrates the major themes of Burns' poetry. The lower section, of a green tint, represents the natural world in which Burns grew up and which is celebrated in his songs and poetry; the middle section, of human figures, represents humanity, again another common theme in Burns' poems, while the top section is a *"sunburst of love"* blossoming *"like a red, red rose"*.

St Giles' Cathedral
High Street
Edinburgh
EH1 1RE
May to September:
Mon–Fri.   9.00–19.00
Sat.   9.00–17.00
Sun.   13.00–17.00
Oct to April: Closes at 17.00 all days
info@stgilescathedral.org.uk
www.stgilescatherdral.org.uk

The Luckenbooths
High Street

When Burns lived in Edinburgh, there were over 80 shops in the Luckenbooths, including one belonging to his publisher, William Creech. Burns would have visited this area on a daily basis.

Inlaid into the cobbles of the High Street adjacent to St Giles', are brass markers. These markers indicate the outline of the site of the Luckenbooths.

A Luckenbooth is a Scottish heart-shaped brooch, given as a token of love or friendship, usually made in silver and often designed as a crown above a heart, or two intertwined hearts. First sold from the 'locked booths', known as the Luckenbooths, on the High Street, they gained popularity from the reign of Mary Queen of Scots (1542–87).

Derived from the old Scots word *Lucken* meaning closed or shut up, these booths were enclosed and capable of being locked.

Dating from 1460, the Luckenbooths were a row of tenements and the city's first permanent shops. Originally 2 high, most had grown to 6 floors in height, some with attic shops by the time they were demolished in 1817 to widen the street, which had been reduced to as little as 15 feet in places.

Below: St Giles' and The Luckenbooths

The tenements connected to the Tolbooth and were built along the north wall of St Giles' almost obscuring the Cathedral from view. This left a narrow space between the Luckenbooths and the walls of St Giles', a space that was taken up with stalls, known as 'Krames' which sold all sorts of goods.

In Robert Burns' time in Edinburgh, there were 81 businesses listed in *Williamson's Directory* working from the Luckenbooths, along with the stalls and the large amount of businesses working from the nearby closes and Parliament Square, the area around St Giles' would have been very busy and almost chaotic.

Amid this bustle, William Creech, Burns' publisher in Edinburgh, attracted daily gatherings in his shop at the east end of the row. Creech had taken ownership of the shop in 1771, and for a further 44 years continued to attract *"clergy, professors and all public and eminent men in the Scottish metropolis"* to his literary lounge which became known as Creech's Levee, although the visitors were also described by some as *"authors and literary idlers."* (see also p.111)

Below: The Luckenbooths

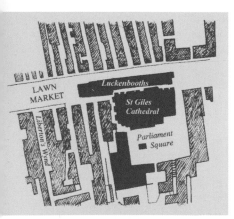

Above: Luckenbooths, from Kincaid's map of 1794

On William Creech

A little upright, pert, tart, tripping wight,
And still his precious Self his dear delight;
Who loves his own smart shadow in the streets
Better than e'er the fairest She he meets.
Much specious lore, but little understood
(Fineering oft outshines the solid wood)
His solid sense by inches you must tell,
But mete his subtle cunning by the ell!
A man of fashion, too, he made his tour,
Learne'd 'Vive la bagatelle et vive l'amour';
So travell'd monkies their grimace improve,
Polish their grin – nay, sigh for ladies' love!
His meddling vanity, a busy friend,
Still making work his Selfish-craft must mend.

Creech's letter comparing 1763 with 1783

William Creech was not only Burns' publisher in Edinburgh but a businessman who was a friend or acquaintance of all in a position of influence in the city. He was a council member, magistrate and provost. He was greatly concerned with the wellbeing of the city and its citizens; in this letter he compares life in Edinburgh in 1763 with that of 1783.

"In 1763 it was fashionable to go to church, and people were interested about religion. Sunday was strictly observed by all ranks as a day of devotion; and it was disgraceful to be seen on the streets during the time of public worship. Families attended church with their children and servants; and family worship was frequent.

"In 1783 attendance on church was greatly neglected, and particularly by the men. Sunday was by many made a day of relaxation; and young people were allowed to stroll about at all hours. Families thought it ungenteel to take their domestics to church with them. The streets were far from being devoid of people in the time of public worship; and, in the evenings, were frequently loose and riotous; particularly to bands of apprentice boys and young lads …

"In no respect were the manners of 1763 and 1783 more remarkable than in the decency, dignity, and delicacy of the one period, compared with the looseness, dissipation, and licentiousness of the other. Many people ceased to blush at what would formerly have been reckoned a crime …

"In 1763 the fines collected by the kirk treasurer for bastard children amounted to £154; and, upon an average of ten successive years, they were £190.

"In 1783 the fines for bastard children amounted to £600, and have since greatly increased …

"In 1763 there were five or six brothels, or houses of bad fame, and a very few of the lowest and most ignorant order of females skulked about the streets at night. A person might have gone from the Castle to Holyrood House (the then length of the city), at any hour in the night, without being accosted by a single street-walker. Street-robbery and pocket-picking were unknown.

"In 1783 the number of brothels had increased twenty-fold, and the women of the town more than a hundred-fold. Every quarter of the city and suburbs was infested with multitudes of females abandoned to vice…

"Street-robbers, pick-pockets, and thieves, had much increased."

William 'Deacon' Brodie

1741–88 Cabinet-maker, criminal

High Street

William Brodie or as he came to be known, Deacon Brodie, was a cabinet-maker, deacon of the trades guild and city councillor of Edinburgh.

He was a highly respectable, and highly respected businessman and an apparent pillar of society. He built up a locksmith's business in the city, and could call on the very highest of city gentry as his customers, working in their homes as well as in their businesses.

He attended many social gatherings where he mixed with the leading members of Edinburgh society.

But he had a secret!

By day, a respectable businessman, by night he used keys he had copied, to rob the very people and businesses that provided him with an honest income.

It is suspected that he began his life as a burglar in 1768 when he used his copied keys to break into a bank, escaping with £800, an enormous sum in those times. His robberies continued, perhaps assuming his position made him beyond suspicion. With two mistresses, numerous children, and gambling debts to finance, in 1786 he recruited three thieves, Brown, Smith and Ainslie.

A robbery in 1786 on an excise office in the Canongate failed and one of the number, Ainslie, was captured. He was 'persuaded' to turn King's Evidence and inform on Brodie and the rest of the gang.

Brodie fled and was traced first to Dunbar, then to Newcastle where he had taken the Flying Mercury Light Coach to York and London. The coachman said that he let down a gentleman answering his description on Old Street, London and from the conversation overheard with other passengers, that they were headed for the continent.

A witness testified that under the guise of another, Brodie had boarded a ship at Blackwall, London, at about 10 o'clock in the evening with 2 others, and that the ship changed course to allow these 3 men to leave the ship at Ostend. A messenger despatched to return him found that he had left Ostend and gone to Amsterdam. He was subsequently traced in Amsterdam where he was imprisoned, eventually being returned to Scotland.

A search of Brodie's house revealed a pair of flintlock pistols buried in the wood yard as well as several picklocks and various pieces of incriminating evidence.

Brodie and Smith were found guilty and hanged at the Tolbooth on 1ˢᵗ October 1788 before a crowd estimated to be over 40,000 strong, ironically using a gallows that Brodie had designed and funded the previous year.

There are several tales of his attempt to cheat the hangman – a flexible pipe down his throat, a steel collar, a harness to take the strain of the rope, and a friendly doctor waiting to revive him! Did he succeed? Did he beat his own efficient gallows? It is very unlikely and he was apparently buried in an unmarked grave at Buccleuch Church in Chapel Street.

But then again, there were soon tales of his being seen in the streets of Europe, and when the coffin was opened to check, it was empty.

It is said that the case inspired Robert Louis Stevenson to write *The Strange Case of Dr Jekyll and Mr Hyde.*

Despite reports stating otherwise, it is unlikely that Burns would have met Brodie. Burns didn't arrive in Edinburgh until late November 1786, by which time Brodie was a wanted man and on the run. He would however have been in Edinburgh shortly after this time and have been aware of the shock and scandal, but at the time of Brodie's trial and hanging, Burns was back in Ayrshire.

William Creech and William Smellie, publisher and printer of Burns' Edinburgh editions, were both named on the prospective jury list with William Creech being chosen as a member of the jury for the trial. Very shortly after the trial, an account written by Creech, *The Trial of William Brodie and George Smith* was published. Creech also had daily reports printed and sold them on the streets of Edinburgh as the trial progressed. Henry Erskine, a fellow member of Lodge Canongate Kilwinning No. 2, was defence counsel for Brodie.

Above: William 'Deacon' Brodie

Left: The two faces of William Brodie, as shown on either side of the sign hanging outside Deacon Brodie's Tavern, on the Royal Mile

James Sibbald

1745–1803 Newspaper editor

High Street

James Sibbald was born in Whitelaw, Roxburghshire, in 1745, the son of a farmer, and was educated in the grammar school of Selkirk. He leased the farm of Newton before eventually selling the business by auction in May 1779, going to Edinburgh with the £100 raised, where he worked for the bookseller Charles Elliot.

In 1781 he purchased the old circulating library which had belonged to Alan Ramsay and was thereafter one of the leading booksellers in Parliament Square. The young Sir Walter Scott was a very regular visitor, "*devouring its contents with ardour*".

He founded the *Edinburgh Magazine* in 1783, and 10 years later, in 1792 he became the editor of the *Edinburgh Herald*. In 1802 he published the literary history *Chronicle of the Poetry of Scotland*.

The October 1786 issue of the *Edinburgh Magazine* contained the very first review of Burns' *Kilmarnock Edition*, stating "*that Burns was a striking example of native genius bursting through the obscurity of poverty …*" Subsequent issues carried excerpts from his poetry, prompting Burns to write in January thanking him.

Below: James Sibbald

Sibbald organised a lease arrangement for the library with a Mr Laurie, which in effect guaranteed Sibbald £200 per annum to be paid quarterly. Sibbald left his business in Edinburgh in 1792, moving to London to pursue a literary career, but returned to Edinburgh in 1797.

Sibbald revised the lease with Laurie to £100 per year, but it did not prosper. The lease reverted back to Sibbald who carried it on until his death.

It was to Sibbald that Patrick Miller of Dalswinton handed £10 for Robert Burns in a philanthropic gesture shortly after Burns' arrival in the city.

Sibbald had been a member of many of the social clubs of Edinburgh, and his birthday was celebrated with a social occasion for many years after his death.

James Sibbald died in Edinburgh in 1803 aged 58, in a lodging house in Leith Walk.

John Kay
1742–1826 Artist
227 High Street

John Kay was born in April 1742 in Dalkeith, near Edinburgh. His father was a stonemason and his mother, the heir to many tenements in Edinburgh and Canongate, was apparently tricked of her inheritance by relatives.

John's youth was traumatic, if his mother's accounts are to be believed. After the death of her husband in 1784, John who was 6 years old was boarded with relatives in Leith. She is convinced they were trying to kill him, short of actual murder. On one occasion he was blown into the sea from a ferry boat, while another time he also fell into the water by falling through a missing board on the pier. Yet again, when he was 'accidentally' pushed overboard, he was dragged out and left for dead only for a sailor to step on his stomach, causing young John to groan loudly and spring back to life.

Even at this young age he showed skill at drawing but was not encouraged and, although he planned to be a mason like his father, he was apprenticed to a Dalkeith barber at the age of 13. Even though he had to do all sorts of menial labour, it was better than his life in Leith and he served here for 6 years.

He came to Edinburgh and served 7 years as a journeyman with various barbers, eventually setting up in business on his own, but only after purchasing his 'freedom of the city' from the Society of Surgeon Barbers on 19th December 1771 at a cost of £40.

Above: John Kay

He lodged with a Mr Nisbet and family, who were to become very good friends and in his leisure time he was able to spend time drawing. When Nisbet died having failed to honour his promise to remember Kay in his will, his son was so grateful for the time that Kay had spent with his father that he made him an annuity of £20 for life.

John Kay then concentrated on building up the artistic side of the business and in 1785 he left the barber's profession.

He was immediately successful, his unique style being very popular. His shop was on the south side of Parliament Square. The shop was destroyed, along with the rest of the old buildings in the square in the great fire of 1824.

Such was Kay's success that there were few people of any prominence in the city who were not to become the focus of his sharp wit and skill on paper. From his shop at 10 Parliament Close, Kay produced around 900 images of the most notable and famous Scotsmen of his time, although, incredibly and sadly, Robert Burns was not one them.

Kay however, did draw many of Burns' contemporaries. He was able to quickly capture, and with some humour, many of those whose images would not otherwise be saved. John Kay's work paints a visual picture of Edinburgh life and society that could otherwise only be guessed at.

While Kay's political views are unknown, it can be surmised from his etchings of those associated with the French Revolution or Liberalism, and his satirical etchings of those in opposition, that Kay may have favoured the Liberal party.

Sadly, not everyone appreciated his caricatures. Some bought them simply to destroy them and on one occasion he was the subject of an unsuccessful prosecution.

A collection of his more artistic drawings is preserved in the library of the Royal Scottish Academy. The department of prints and drawings in the British Museum has his book, completed after his death, *A Complete Collection of the Portraits and Caricatures, Drawn and Engraved by John Kay, Edinburgh, from the Year 784 to 1713.*

His work can also be viewed in the Scottish National Portrait Gallery, Edinburgh, and the Metropolitan Museum in New York.

He was married twice, first when he was aged 20, to Lily Steven who bore him 10 children, all of whom, with the exception of William, died in infancy. Lily died in 1785. He then married Margaret Scott in 1787.

He was described as a slender, straight old man, of middle size and *"antique cut"* clothes, with quiet, unassuming manners.

John Kay died on 21st February 1826 at No. 227 High Street, Edinburgh, aged 84 and is buried in Greyfriars Kirkyard.

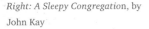

Right: A Sleepy Congregation, by John Kay

Lord William Craig
1745–1813 Judge, cousin of Agnes McLehose

High Street

William Craig was the son of a Glasgow minister, also William, and a cousin of Agnes McLehose. He was an advocate and Sheriff Depute of Ayr. In 1792 he was raised to the bench as Lord Craig and was made a judge in 1795.

Craig and other advocates were members of a literary society called the Tabernacle. They met to read and discuss essays they had written. Craig suggested that they publish their work, the society's name was changed to the Mirror Club and the publication was called *The Mirror*. It was published by William Creech twice-weekly from January 1799 to May 1781.

When Agnes became separated from her husband and her annuities were stopped, Craig stepped in and looked after her financially. However Craig didn't like Burns and Agnes always had to be careful that gossip about her and Burns did not reach her cousin's ears.

On one occasion she was warned by Craig and the Reverend Kemp, that rumours were circulating about a relationship. Fortunately for Agnes, they didn't know the man in question was Burns!

Craig was a literary fellow of the Royal Society of Edinburgh, also serving as Rector of Glasgow University from 1801–03.

Above. Lord William Craig

For all of his life Craig looked after Agnes' wellbeing. When a dispute over publication of some of the Clarinda letters reached the Court of Session in 1804, Lord Craig gave one of the longest opinions. It is thought that his astute reading of all the factors in a legally complex case persuaded fellow lords and helped win the day for Burns' family, enabling Agnes to remain on the sidelines, free of scandal, her reputation intact.

In his will he left his library and a substantial sum of money to Andrew, the sole survivor of Agnes' four children. He also left Agnes an annuity which secured her financially.

In his private life he was loved for his gentle, unassuming manners and benevolent, sociable personality. Lord William Craig died at his home in York Place on 8th July 1813, aged 68, and is buried in Canongate Kirkyard.

John McLaurin, Lord Dreghorn

1734–96 Advocate

High Street

John McLaurin was a second cousin of Agnes, on her mother's side, and he treated Agnes poorly. He was described by biographer James Mackay as a *"petty, vindictive, morose hypocrite"* who gave his cousin no help and refused to even acknowledge her. It was left to Lord William Craig to care and look after her.

He was an advocate who was appointed a senator of the College of Justice in 1788 and took the title Lord Dreghorn. He was also a writer and the author of *The Philosopher's Opera* which he wrote at Dreghorn Castle, Colinton.

He was obsessed with cleaning up Edinburgh by closing down all its brothels in 1789. This, of course, incurred Burns' wrath.

In August of that year, a complaint was raised by neighbours against two prostitutes, one whom went by the name of Margaret Burns, for running an *"irregular and disorderly house …"* Miss Burns' real surname was Matthews. She was originally from Durham, and became a young high-class prostitute who lived in Rose Street.

She was well-known in the area, attracting the attention of artist John Kay who sketched her dressed in her usual attractive and extravagantly beautiful clothes.

William Creech was chair of the city magistrates and it was decided that the 2 women were to be banished from the city of Edinburgh for life.

They petitioned their case at the Court of Session to the Lord Ordinary, Lord Dreghorn who refused the appeal.

Miss Burns, represented by Robert Burns' friend Henry Erskine, appealed to the Inner House and the case was found in her favour on 22nd December 1789.

Lifelong bachelor William Creech was incensed when a London newspaper announced that *"Bailie Creech, of literary celebrity in Edinburgh, was about to lead the beautiful and accomplished Miss Burns to the hymeneal altar."*

Creech demanded a retraction and apology. The apology which followed was worse than the original slander: *"matters having been otherwise arranged to the mutual satisfaction of both parties and their respective friends"*, suggesting that Creech and Miss Burns were having an affair.

Margaret Burns died only 2 years or so later, aged 23, at Roslin in 1792.

Robert Burns followed the case and in a letter to Peter Hill said: *"How is the fate of my poor Mademoiselle Burns decided? … as for those flinty-bosomed, puritanical Prosecutors of Female Frailty, and Prosecutors of Female Charms … it is written that 'Thou shalt not take the name of the Lord thy God in vain', so I shall neither say, G— curse them! Nor G— damn them! But may Woman curse them! May Woman blast them! May Woman damn them!"*

Written under the Portrait of the Celebrated Miss Burns

Cease, ye *prudes,* your envious railing,
Lovely Burns has charms – *confess;*
True it is, she had one failing,
Had ae woman ever less?

Peter Hill

1754–1837 Bookseller

Parliament Square

This was the location of the bookshop of Peter Hill, who helped his friend Burns with finances. Peter Williamson opened a coffee shop here on his return to Edinburgh.

Above: Peter Hill

Peter Hill was born in Dysart, Fife in 1754.

When Burns met him in 1787 he was a clerk in Creech's bookshop in the High Street. Hill left Creech in 1788 and set up his own bookshop in Parliament Square.

By 1793 Hill had moved his bookshop to The Cross of Edinburgh with his home at Ramsay Garden. He was also Treasurer of Edinburgh City Council and Heriot's Hospital.

Hill's wife, Elizabeth Lindsay, did not approve of Robert Burns, but this does not seem to have affected the friendship of the two men.

Burns wrote many letters to Peter Hill, not only conducting a variety of business matters via the eve-helpful Hill, but also confiding personal matters to him.

Many of the letters were orders for books, some for himself, but many were orders made on behalf of the lending, or circulating, library he had set up with Robert Riddell. Riddell had organised a friendly society among his local farmers and workers, and the Monkland Friendly Society Library was founded in March 1789 with Burns as organiser and treasurer. This inspired local library lasted well beyond the death of its founders until 2nd February 1931!

Hill stayed at 160 Nicolson Street, adjacent to St Patrick's Square. He moved to Ramsay Garden by 1793. Peter Hill died in 1837, aged 83.

Peter Williamson, 'Indian Peter'

1730–99 Started the Penny Post

Parliament Square

Nicknamed 'Indian Peter', Williamson was a colourful character. He was born in Aboyne, near Aberdeen in 1730.

When he was 13 years old, Peter was staying with his aunt and while playing at Aberdeen harbour was abducted by two men and taken to a barn. These kidnap gangs roamed all over the countryside and took the captured children to The Green, at the foot of the large steps on Union Street, Aberdeen – a building that was used to house slave boys until they were shipped off abroad. These kidnapper's houses employed the service of a piper to play the bagpipes so that the noise would drown out the sounds of the children.

Seventeenth-century authorities all over Britain had decided to get vandals and young waifs and strays off their streets by sending them to the colonies in the guise of offering an indentured servitude, which in reality was no more than an officially sanctioned slave trade in children.

Peter ended up on a ship, the *Planter*, and after an 11-week voyage he was sold to another Scot, Hugh Williamson, who had Peter work on his farm. When Wilson died 4 years later, he left Peter a large sum of money and a horse in his will, leaving Peter a free man.

On his travels he fell in love and married a planter's daughter in Pennsylvania but when Delaware Indians attacked the house he was taken prisoner. He was tortured and became a slave to them before managing to escape after 3 months, making his way home only to discover his wife had died 2 months previously.

With the loss of his wife Peter had no desire to continue farming and joined the Pennsylvania Volunteers in the battle against the French. Deep into enemy territory he was captured by the French on the British surrender in 1756.

Finally, he was repatriated from Quebec in a prisoner exchange and was returned to Plymouth, England, where he was invalided from the army because of his injuries.

From Plymouth he went to York where he published his memoirs. Promoting book sales by dressing up in headdress and war paint, smoking a peace pipe and doing war dances, he earned the nickname of Indian Peter.

Fifteen years after being kidnapped he returned to Aberdeen not only to find his family, but also set up an exhibition of Indian culture and exposed the Aberdeen child-slavery scandal. He was soon arrested for libel after accusing civic officials of being behind the trade and he was jailed, fined and eventually banished from the town.

Moving to Edinburgh, where he regularly walked the streets in full Delaware

Indian costume, one of his first enterprises was to open a coffee shop in Parliament Square. Here he met and became friendly with many lawyers and others in the legal profession and learning Scots law himself, soon had the knowledge and confidence to take the case to the Court of Session where, after a 6-year court battle, won his case and substantial damages.

Partly backed by this cash he set up several enterprises, most notably the first Edinburgh Penny Post in 1773, which was to carry the Sylvander/ Clarinda letters. He used a network of local shops as collection points and in 1787, one office was in Register House, next to St James Square, and another, run by a Mrs Anderson, was in Chapel Street on the corner of Potterrow, very near to Agnes' house. Letters deposited at a collection point would be delivered within the hour from 9am until 9pm.

Left: Peter Williamson and James Bruce, Esq of Kinnaird (pointing)

Very soon, there were so many letters coming and going between the two that Agnes was afraid the liason with Burns would be exposed to all and instead used her maid Jenny Clow to carry the letters. A decision she, and Jenny, were to soon regret.

Among other ventures, Peter also started *Williamson's Street Directory,* one of the world's first street directories, which ran for 10 years before being bought over by the General Post Office.

It is thought that his story inspired the novels of James Fenimore Cooper, who wrote *The Last of the Mohicans,* and also inspired Robert Louis Stevenson's *Kidnapped.*

Peter Williamson became addicted to alcohol and on the 9th January 1799, aged 69, he was buried in his Delaware Indian clothes. His unmarked grave lies to the north-east of the Martyr's Monument in the Old Calton Burial Ground.

Lawnmarket

1 Wardrop's Court

2 Lady Stair's Close

3 Ramsay Garden

4 White Hart Inn

5 Greyfriars Kirk

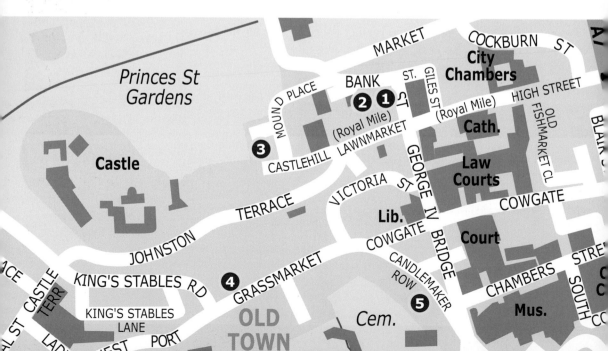

Wardrop's Court
451 Lawnmarket, EH1 2NT

It was here in Wardrop's Court that Robert Burns sat several times for Alexander Nasmyth as he completed the portrait that was to adorn the *Edinburgh Edition* of Burns' poems.

Below: Geddes Dragon, Wardrop's Court

Bottom: Wardrop's Court Entrance

Wardrop's Court, once called Middle Baxter's Court, lies to the east of Lady Stair's Close and was formed following the demolition of tenements which once separated the court from Patterson's Court.

Burns stayed nearby in Baxter's Close with a window that overlooked Lady Stair's courtyard; this was one of the tenements demolished in the 1890s. Several of the original closes in this area were cleared away during the construction of Bank Street.

Wardrop's Court archway is 'guarded over' by four ornate dragons. The Lawnmarket Dragons, carved by J.S. Gibson are more ornate and detailed than those on the court side, known as the Geddes Dragons and carved by Arthur Geddes, son of Sir Patrick Geddes.

The dragons were renovated by Edinburgh World Heritage and brought back to their former glory in 2012. At one time painted green, the dragons have been returned to their original blue colour with gilding.

Patrick Geddes was a town planner and

Right: Wardrop's Court

conservationist, described as a man ahead of his time, who developed a method called 'Conservative Surgery' for the regeneration of inner-city Edinburgh. The creation of Makar's Court at Lady Stair's Close is a direct result of Geddes' principles which were practised throughout the city.

As Burns' fame grew, Alexander Nasmyth quickly became a household name as for many years his portrait was the only available image of Burns. It became one of the most copied paintings ever; when owned by Burns' sons after the death of Jean, they would take the painting to various Burns meetings and gatherings, allowing anyone who wanted the opportunity to examine and copy it.

Nasmyth himself made three copies, one of which is in the Portrait Gallery in London, one is in Kelvingrove Art Gallery and Museum in Glasgow and the other, known as the Shaw Burns and discovered in 2011, is in private hands.

Site of Baxter's Close

Burns lodged here on his very first visit to Edinburgh. A plaque commemorates this at the location of the original house.

Baxter's Close is one of four close names for the property of the Incorporation of Baxters (Bakers) which stood 200 feet north of the High Street on a site now occupied by North Bank Street.

Burns stayed with his friend, Ayrshire born John Richmond, a lawyer's clerk, in Mrs Carfae's residence.

The room was rented for 18 pence a week and came with "*a deal table, a sanded floor and a chaff bed.*" It was situated over a brothel which kept the lodgers awake at night.

There was an order of society in these tenement buildings, which often reached 10 stories high. Those who could pay more stayed on the upper floors. The more money you had, the further away it took you from the foul smells of the street.

The landlady was very upset by the loose living going on downstairs by neighbours who, in her own words, "*lie up gandygoing with their filthy fellows, drinking the best of wines, and singing abominable songs. They shall one day die in hell, weeping and wailing and gnashing their teeth over a cup of God's wrath.*"

Burns' room, with a single window, looked out into Lady Stair's courtyard. He stayed here from 28th November 1786 until 5th May 1787.

ADDRESS TO EDINBURGH.

[This universally admired piece could not fail to assist in giving the poet's name a *lift* in the Scottish capital. He has omitted to notice none of the specialities of which Edinburgh is so justly proud, not even its charitable institutions being passed over without a compliment. He enclosed this poem along with another piece unnamed, to Mr. William Chalmers, writer, Ayr, so early as 27th Dec., 1786, thus showing the rapidity with which he had composed it; for he had then been only three weeks in the city. He says, "I enclose you two poems, which I have carded and spun since I passed Glenbuck. One blank in the *Address to Edinburgh*, 'Fair B——,' is heavenly Miss Burnet, daughter to Lord Monboddo, at whose house I have had the honour to be more than once. There has not been anything nearly like her in all the combinations of beauty, grace, and goodness the Creator has formed, since Milton's Eve on the first day of her existence." This beautiful creature died in 1789.

Left: Introduction to *Address to Edinburgh*, from *Burns' Complete Works*, Kilmarnock Edition (Life & Notes by Wm. Scott Douglas)

Address to Edinburgh

Edina! Scotia's darling seat!
All hail thy palaces and tow'rs,
Where once beneath a Monarch's feet,
Sat Legislation's sov'reign pow'rs!
From marking wildly-scatt'red flow'rs,
As on the banks of Ayr I stray'd,
And singing, lone, the ling'ring hours,
I shelter in thy honour'd shade.

Here Wealth still swells the golden tide,
As busy Trade his labours plies;
There Architecture's noble pride
Bids elegance and splendour rise:
Here Justice, from her native skies,
High wields her balance and her rod;
There Learning, with his eagle eyes,
Seeks Science in her coy abode.

Thy sons, Edina, social, kind,
With open arms the stranger hail;
Their views enlarg'd, their lib'ral mind,
Above the narrow, rural vale:
Attentive still to Sorrow's wail,
Or modest Merit's silent claim;
And never may their sources fail!
And never envy blot their name!

Thy daughters bright thy walks adorn,
Gay as the gilded summer sky,
Sweet as the dewy, milk-white thorn,
Dear as the raptur'd thrill of joy!
Fair Burnet strikes th' adoring eye,
Heav'n's beauties on my fancy shine;
I see the Sire of Love on high,
And own His work indeed divine!

There, watching high the least alarms,
Thy rough, rude fortress gleams afar;
Like some bold vet'ran, grey in arms,
And mark'd with many a seamy scar:
The pond'rous wall and massy bar,
Grim-rising o'er the rugged rock,
Have oft withstood assailing war,
And oft repell'd th' Invader's shock.

With awe-struck thought, and pitying tears,
I view that noble, stately Dome,
Where Scotia's kings of other years,
Fam'd heroes! had their royal home:
Alas, how chang'd the times to come!
Their royal name low in the dust!
Their hapless race wild-wand'ring roam!
Tho' rigid Law cries out 'twas just!

Wild-beats my heart to trace your steps,
Whose ancestors, in days of yore,
Thro' hostile ranks and ruin'd gaps
Old Scotia's bloody lion bore:
Ev'n I who sing in rustic lore,
Haply my Sires have left their shed,
And fac'd grim Danger's loudest roar,
Bold – following where your fathers led!

Edina! Scotia's darling seat!
All hail thy palaces and tow'rs,
Where once, beneath a Monarch's feet,
Sat Legislation's sov'reign pow'rs:
From marking wildly-scatt'red flow'rs,
As on the banks of Ayr I stray'd,
And singing, lone, the ling'ring hours,
I shelter in thy honor'd shade.

The Writers' Museum
Lady Stair's Close, Lawnmarket, EH1 2PA

The Writers' Museum is a celebration of the works of Burns, Scott and Stevenson. Much of Edinburgh City's collection of Burns artefacts are housed here.

Right: The Writers' Museum

The building which now houses The Writers' Museum was begun around 1622 by Sir William Gray. When he died, the close was named Lady Gray's Close after his widow. By the 1720s, the somewhat altered house was owned by Elizabeth, Dowager-Countess of Stair and the close and house were renamed after her. She also owned an estate in Mauchline, Ayrshire,

Lady Stair was regarded as the queen of Edinburgh society when she died in November 1759. Thirty years later in 1789 the house was advertised for sale for the sum of £250.

In 1895 the fifth Earl of Roseberry, a descendant of Sir William Gray, saved the house from demolition and, after restoration, the earl presented the building to the city of Edinburgh to be used as a museum.

Lady Stair's House has been the Museum of Edinburgh History (1907–32) and was the Museum of Childhood (now in the High Street) until 1956.

The city had been amassing a collection of Burns' artefacts for many years, housing them in various locations including the Burns Monument, before it was decided to bring the pieces together and house the majority of the collection at Lady Stair's. With the addition of items relating to Sir Walter Scott and Robert Louis Stevenson, the museum was renamed The Writers' Museum in 1993.

There is a fascinating and varied collection of Burns' related objects to be found here. Personal letters and items owned by Burns and his family; Burns' draft of *Scots Wha Hae* and the stool that Burns sat on for many months while he corrected proofs at Smellie's printing works are just a few of the objects on view.

Not to be missed is the Taylor portrait, the first portrait that Burns ever sat for. Remarkably, in an Edinburgh that boasted some of the finest artists in Britain, Taylor was one of only three artists that Robert Burns did sit for.

Another fine portrait, much larger, and by an unknown artist, depicts a young Robert Burns surrounded by items of his craft. This contemporary painting was donated to the museum about 1960–62.

As well as housing an important collection of Burns work The Writers' Museum has also a very good collection of Burns-related items associated with people who he knew very well in Edinburgh.

In recent times, the courtyard has become known as the Makars' Court, which celebrates the work of Scottish writers in the form of inlaid paving tiles inscribed with quotations from their work. These tiles follow the path through the courtyard to the High Street. The courtyard may also be accessed from Market Street/North Bank Street, but from that side there are stairs and an incline which makes it unsuitable for wheelchairs or those with restricted mobility.

Below: Lady Stair's Close. A footnote in Cassell's *Old and New Edinburgh* indicates that the window at the right of the illustration is that of the room occupied by Burns.

Jean Lorimer
1775–1831 Friend
Lawnmarket

One of the relics held by The Writers Museum is a lock of Jean Lorimer's hair. She is the famous *"lassie wi' the Lint-white locks"* from Burns' song. The lock was gifted by Robert Chambers, Burns' biographer, who obtained it from Jean's sister.

Jean Lorimer was born at Craigieburn, near Moffat in 1755, the eldest daughter of William Lorimer and Agnes Carson.

Jean Lorimer was about 15 years old when she first met Burns. Her father was a farmer and merchant, dealing in teas and spirits, a combination that brought him to the attention of Burns in his job as an exciseman. He became great friends with Jean's father and Robert and Jean Armour were invited to dine with the Lorimers at Kemys Hall near Dumfries many times. Invitations were reciprocated and Jean Lorimer visited Mrs Burns in Dumfries often.

Below: Jean Lorimer

There is no doubt that Robert was attracted to her, and although gossips allege that they had an affair, Robert denied this, writing to George Thomson on 19th October 1794, urging him to accept the song *Craigieburnwood* in his selection as *"The Lady on whom it is made, is one of the finest women in Scotland, & in fact (entre nous) is in a manner to me what Sterne's Eliza was to him – a Mistress, or Friend, or what you will, in the guileless simplicity of Platonic love"*. Burns goes on to chastise Thomson not to *"put any squinting construction on this"* and reminds him that *"to my lovely friend you are indebted for many of your best songs of mine"*.

In the same letter, Burns explains that *"to be more than ordinary in song"* he *"puts himself in the regimen of admiring a fine woman; & in proportion to the adorability of her charms, in proportion you are delighted with my verses"*.

In 1794 Burns would have been aged 35 and Jean aged 19. Regardless of whether or not there was a sexual liaison between them, Burns gave Jean the name of Chloris, meaning Goddess of Flowers, a name she is recognised by to this day. Between 1793–95, the young and beautiful Chloris inspired him to pen at least 24 songs.

Burns wasn't the only man who was attracted to Jean. His fellow excise officer, John Gillespie was deeply smitten, along with several of the young men of the area, however she accepted an offer of marriage from Andrew Whelpdale, and ran off to Gretna Green to marry him in 1773.

The marriage with Whelpdale was disastrous. Only weeks into the marriage he had used up her money and abandoned her, forcing her return to her parents, penniless, married, and not yet 19 years old.

Around 1794 her father's business failed and he lost everything. When he died senile in 1808 Jean was now homeless with no means of support. For many years she lived an itinerant life, some say the life of a vagrant and there are reports that she was forced to turn to prostitution. The biographer Chambers wrote, *"it is understood that this poor unprotected woman at length was led into an error which lost her the respect of society"*.

However, in 1825 her plight was highlighted by an unnamed gentleman in Edinburgh newspapers and her connection with Burns ensured public sympathy. Through the charitable gentleman's wife, Jean found herself with a job as housekeeper to a gentleman in the Blacket Place area of Newington and even when she took ill, he found her lodgings in Middleton Entry, supporting her there until she died in September 1831, aged 56.

She is buried in East Preston Street Cemetery, her grave marked with a Celtic Cross erected by the Ninety Burns Club, Edinburgh, 1901.

Lassie wi' the lintwhite locks

Lassie wi' the lintwhite locks,
Bonie lassie, artless lassie,
Wilt thou wi' me tent the flocks,
An wilt thou be my Dearie O?

Now Nature cleeds the flowery lea,
And a' is young and sweet like thee,
O wilt thou share its joys wi' me,
And say thou'lt be my Dearie O.

The primrose bank, the wimpling burn,
The cuckoo on the milkwhite thorn,
The wanton lambs at rosy morn
Shall glad thy heart, my Dearie, O.

And when the welcome simmer shower
Has chear'd ilk drooping little flower,
We'll to the breathing woodbine bower
At sultry noon, my Dearie, O.

When Cynthia lights, wi' silver ray,
The weary shearer's hameward way,
Thro' yellow waving fields we'll stray,
And talk o' love, my Dearie, O.

And should the howling wintry blast
Disturb my lassie's midnight rest,
I'll fauld thee to my faithfu' breast,
And comfort thee, my Dearie O.

Lassie wi' the lintwhite locks,
Bonie lassie, artless lassie,
Wilt thou wi' me tent the flocks,
An wilt thou be my Dearie O?

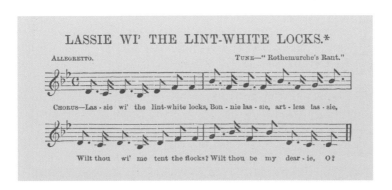

LASSIE WI' THE LINT-WHITE LOCKS.*

ALLEGRETTO.   TUNE—"Rothemurche's Rant."

CHORUS—Las-sie wi' the lint-white locks, Bon-nie las-sie, art-less las-sie,

Wilt thou wi' me tent the flocks? Wilt thou be my dear-ie, O?

George Thomson
1757–1851 Collector of songs
Lawnmarket

George Thomson was born in Limekilns in Fife in 1757. He wanted, like Johnson, to collect Scottish songs. His first disastrous partner in this venture was Andrew Erskine, who committed suicide in 1793 when he drowned himself in the Forth, because he could not face up to bankruptcy.

Thomson loved Burns' *Cotter's Saturday Night* and wrote to Burns about the new collection he was planning, the *Select Collection of Scottish Airs*: "*To render this work perfect, we are desirous to have the poetry improved wherever it seems unworthy of the music.*"

Burns was commissioned to write 20–25 songs to melodies for, as usual, no pay. Burns felt that is was his God-given duty to save and assist in the collection of these songs and melodies for Scotland's heritage and steadfastly refused payment, even at times when he dearly needed the funds.

When Thomson sent him money Burns replied in July 1793, "*I assure you, my dear Sir, that you truly hurt me with your pecuniary parcel. It degrades me in my own eyes. However to return it would savour of affectation; but, as to any more traffic of that debtor and creditor kind, I swear by the HONOUR which crowns the upright statue of ROBERT BURNS'S INTEGRITY – on the least notion of it, I will indignantly spurn the bypast transaction, and from that moment commence to be an entire stranger to you!*"

When Burns was dying, in a letter to Thomson on the 12th July 1796 from Brow on the Solway Firth where Burns was being treated, he reluctantly asked Thomson for £5. Thomson replied immediately on the 14th saying that he had been thinking of ways to help but was mindful of Burns' previous warnings. Thomson wrote, "*I thank you heartily therefore for the frankness of your letter of the 12th, and with great pleasure inclose a draft for the very sum I proposed sending. Would I be chancellor of the Exchequer but for one day, for your sake!*"

In 1795, Thomson surprised Burns by sending him a gift of David Allan's sketch of *A Cotter's Saturday Night* a gesture that delighted Burns as Allan had painted Burns into the scene as the Cotter's son. Burns wrote, "*… My fiz is sae kenspeckle, that the very joiner's apprentice, whom Mrs Burns employed to break up the parcel (I was out of town that day), knew it at once. My most grateful compliments to Alan, who has honoured my rustic muse so much with his masterly pencil.*"

After Burns' death the picture was gifted around July 1799 to Mrs Dunlop of Dunlop by Gilbert Burns, on behalf of Jean Armour, in an apparent gesture of recognition for the help, advice and encouragement Mrs Dunlop had given Burns over many years. Burns corresponded more with Mrs Dunlop than with any other person. She had become upset with Burns' insensitivity in political matters and the correspondence stopped, but one of the last letters that Burns read before he died was a conciliatory letter from Mrs Dunlop.

As well as the invaluable contribution of Burns to his collection of Scottish songs, Thomson also managed to secure the involvement of such internationally famous musicians as Haydn, Weber, and even Beethoven.

Thomson was an arrogant and poor editor of Burns' lyrics, also altering Burns' letters, which had the effect of distorting information in early biographies of the poet. Thomson also edited Beethoven's music!

Burns was several times frustrated at Thomson's attempts to alter his words, replying on one occasion, June 1793, Burns writes, *"I cannot alter the disputed lines in the 'Mill mill, O'' What you think a defect, I esteem as a positive beauty; so you see how doctors differ."*

However, Thomson finally made some amends by raising money for the Burns Monument and is said to have accommodated Jean on her second visit to Edinburgh. His portrait in The Writers' Museum is by Colum Smith.

Thomson also owned a copy of Nasmyth's portrait of Burns, most likely the last of the three copies made. After Thomson's death his son William, sold the portrait as being the work of Alexander Nasmyth, with assistance by Henry Raeburn. The Raeburn connection has always been disputed and the portrait is now in the National Portrait Gallery in London, credited as the work of Alexander Nasmyth. It was among only 57 items which made up the collection on the opening of the gallery in 1859.

Thomson retired and moved to London in 1839. In a letter to his son he wrote that the London streets frightened him and were too dangerous for a man of his years. After his wife died in 1841, he moved to the quieter Brighton. However, he wrote, *"I am weary of Brighton, where there are handsome buildings no doubt, but little else to look at, except the sea, without ships, which are only to be seen dimly in the far offing as they pass up and down the channel: no meadows, gardens, plantations, shrubberies, or any rural scenery, which I long to see again."* He returned to Edinburgh in 1845.

Below: George Thomson

One of Thomson's grand-daughters, Catherine Hogarth, was the wife of the author Charles Dickens who lived for a time in Edinburgh. Dickens composed the epitaph on Thomson's tombstone, a service Burns had once done for Robert Fergusson.

Thomson died in Leith on 18th February 1851, two weeks before his 94th birthday, and is buried in Kensal Green Cemetery, London, alongside his wife.

Allan Ramsay, Snr
c1685–1758 Bookseller
Ramsay Garden

Allan Ramsay played a large and important part in establishing the foundations of the Scottish literary tradition and the bridge between the great 'makars' of the 15th and 16th centuries, inspiring the genius of his greater successors Robert Fergusson, Robert Burns and Walter Scott.

Ramsay had died 28 years before Burns' first came to Edinburgh, but one of the first places Burns visited was where Allan Ramsay had operated his bookselling and library businesses. Creech, publisher of the *Edinburgh Edition*, had taken over Allan Ramsay's premises in the Luckenbooths, the ramshackle building beside the north wall of St Giles' High Kirk. It was to Creech's establishment that Burns was to come regularly.

Ramsay was a wig maker originally, apprenticed in Edinburgh in 1701, but became a Scottish poet (or makar), and was also a playwright, publisher, editor and librarian.

He published his own poetry, and a variety of transcripts such as *Christ's Kirk on the Green* from *The Bannatyne Manuscript*, (1716) an anthology of literature compiled in Scotland in the 16th century, originally collected by the Edinburgh merchant George Bannatyne, with some additions of his own. In turn, Ramsay added some of his own work. He became fully occupied in writing verse and collecting and editing older Scots literature, and in 1724 he published the first volume of *Tea-Table Miscellany*, an influential collection of Scottish song. In the same year, his *The Ever Green* collected work of the medieval and 17th-century Makars.

He corresponded with William Hamilton of Bangour, William Somervile, John Gay and Alexander Pope and opened the first circulating library in Britain whilst developing his business as a bookseller from the Luckenbooths.

Below: Allan Ramsay, Snr

Ramsay enjoyed success as a writer, and was famous during his lifetime as author of the Scots pastoral play, *The Gentle Shepherd*, which was published in 1725. but his importance was as an editor, reviving the interest in vernacular literature. Without Ramsay, many Scottish works would have been lost.

Ramsay was also a great supporter of the stage, writing for London theatres. In 1736 he built a new theatre in Carruber's Close, Edinburgh, but there was severe opposition from extremists in the Presbytery of the Church of Scotland and the venture closed in 1737. Ramsay had acquired land at Castle Hill, Edinburgh, and, helped by his son, designed, built and retired to the 8-sided house, Ramsay Lodge, (nicknamed 'The Goosedub', or 'Goose Pie', by his contemporaries) which then looked over fields, but now looks out over Princes Street and the New Town to the north from Ramsay Garden.

He remained active until his death 1758. Ramsay is buried at Greyfriars Kirkyard, Edinburgh.

Ramsay's House
Ramsay Garden, EH1 2NA

The surrounding houses in Ramsay Garden were developed much later (between 1890 and 1893) by Sir Patrick Geddes who was responsible for urban renewal in the Old Town area.

Geddes (1854–1932) was a botanist by training making his name through his discovery of chlorophyll, the natural pigment of all plants, before studying the influences on human behaviour of biology and environment and new strategies for city planning. His theories recognised the significance of history on the everyday behaviour of a town's inhabitants, and his work on Ramsay Garden was an early product of his vision. The area had fallen into disrepair, and Geddes hoped both to improve the living conditions of the working class, and to increase the number of wealthier residents.

Geddes employed the architect Stewart Henbest Capper to remodel Ramsay Lodge, and to extend it with six new flats built onto it at right angles. The work was then overseen by Sydney Mitchell, who took over as architect. The result was a combination of traditional Scottish domestic architecture with the addition of balconies and towers to form Ramsay Garden, which is now a block of apartment buildings that overlook Princes Street Gardens and are an iconic feature of the city's skyline.

Allan Ramsay, Jnr (1713–84) was the son of Allan Ramsay the poet. Born in Edinburgh he studied art in Rome and London returning to Edinburgh establishing himself as a portrait painter. He moved to London and became part of the intellectual society of the day before retiring to Dover where he died on August 10th, 1784. The National Portrait Galleries in both London and Edinburgh have examples of his work.

Below: Ramsay Lodge

Bottom: Ramsay Garden from Princes Street

White Hart Inn
32 Grassmarket, EH1 2JU

Robert Burns stayed here when he had to come to Edinburgh in November 1791 to see Jenny Clow, the former servant to Mrs Agnes McLehose. Clarinda (Mrs McLehose) seeking to keep the Clarinda and Sylvander correspondence secret, rather than use the postal service, had sent Jenny to deliver a letter to Robert Burns, who seduced her. Twenty-year-old Jenny gave birth to Burns' child, Robert Burns Clow in Edinburgh in 1788.

Above: Grassmarket, 1794

Robert Ainslie had written to tell Robert about Jenny's condition, just a year after writing a similar letter to Burns regarding May Cameron. In his reply the poet wrote, *"I am vexed at that affair of the girl, but dare not enlarge on the subject until you send me direction, as I suppose that will be altered on your late Master and Friend's death."*

Robert Burns was willing to take Jenny's baby into his home, but his mother would not part with him.

On 6th January 1789 a letter written by Burns to Robert Ainslie makes it clear that Jenny Clow had in fact served Burns with a writ and that he intended to travel to Edinburgh, to *"settle that matter with her, and free her hand of the process"*.

It was whilst he was in Dumfries in November of 1791, three years after the birth of the child, that Robert Burns received a letter from Agnes McLehose, who informed him, bluntly, that Jenny Clow *"to all appearances is at this moment dying. Obliged, from all the symptoms of a rapid decay, to quit her service, she is gone to a room almost without common necessaries, untended and unmourned. In circumstances so distressing, to whom can she so naturally look for aid as to the father of her child, the man for whose sake she has suffered many a sad and anxious night, shut from the world, with no other companions than guilt and solitude? You have now an opportunity to evince you indeed possess those fine feelings you have delineated, so as to claim the just admiration of your country. I am convinced I need add nothing farther to persuade you to act as every consideration of humanity must dictate."*

Burns replied and asked that Mrs McLehose arrange to get five shillings to Jenny Clow on his behalf, promising to repay her on his arrival and then made arrangements to take a week's leave from his excise duties and travel to Edinburgh.

On 29th November 1791, Burns arrived at The White Hart Inn. He stayed for a week and met with Jenny within a few hours, giving her an undisclosed sum of money. There are no records of any financial or other arrangements made at that time.

At the end of November Clarinda accepted an invitation from her husband in Jamaica to join him there and in the belief that she was about to leave the country forever she consented to receive a parting visit from Burns – the meeting took place on 6th December 1791. They exchanged locks of hair and never saw each other again.

From Dumfries on the 27th December, 1791, Burns sent Clarinda *Ae Fond Kiss* – one of the most poignant love songs ever written.

Jenny died from tuberculosis 2 months after the visit from Burns, just 3 years after giving birth. Her son later became a wealthy merchant in London, and he in turn married and had a son, also Robert Burns Clow – given his father's names, customary at the time.

The inn was the chief place for carriers to stay in the days when all traffic was by cart or wagon. Around 50 carriers arrived weekly in The Grassmarket at the time when Burns stayed, a noisy and crowded part of the city. Not far from the inn was the gallows where public hangings took place until 1784.

The inn has a long history, dating from the 1500s. The present building dates from 1740 and is Edinburgh's oldest continually used public house.

Many famous people have stayed here over the years including Dorothy and William Wordsworth.

Above: The White Hart Inn

Around 1828 William Burke and William Hare used the inn to target many of their victims, following them before smothering them with a pillow (now known as 'burking') and selling the bodies to Professor Robert Knox, a lecturer of anatomy at the university. They committed at least 16 murders, and possibly as many as 30.

Below: Burke and Hare

Hare gave evidence against Burke and escaped prosecution while Burke was found guilty on Christmas morning 1828. He was hanged on 28th January 1829 in front of an estimated crowd of 25,000. The following day his body was publicly dissected.

The artists impressions here of Burke and Hare, by David Alexander, are based on the death mask of Burke, a life mask of Hare and court sketches taken during the trial. The mask of Hare is on display at Edinburgh University's Anatomy Museum and copies of both can be found in the Scottish National Portrait Gallery.

Unsurprisingly, the inn is reportedly the most haunted in Scotland.

Ae Fond Kiss

Ae fond kiss, and then we sever;
Ae fareweel, and then for ever!
Deep in heart-wrung tears I'll pledge thee,
Warring sighs and groans I'll wage thee.
Who shall say that Fortune grieves him,
While the star of hope she leaves him?
Me, nae cheerful twinkle lights me;
Dark despair around benights me.

I'll ne'er blame my partial fancy,
Naething could resist my Nancy:
But to see her was to love her;
Love but her, and love for ever.
Had we never lov'd sae kindly,
Had we never lov'd sae blindly,
Never met or never parted,
We had ne'er been broken-hearted.

Fare-thee-weel, thou first and fairest!
Fare-thee-weel, thou best and dearest!
Thine be ilka joy and treasure,
Peace, Enjoyment, Love and Pleasure!
Ae fond kiss, and then we sever!
Ae fareweel alas, for ever!
Deep in heart-wrung tears I'll pledge thee,
Warring sighs and groans I'll wage thee.

Greyfriars Kirkyard
88 Candlemaker Row, EH1 2QA

Many friends and acquaintances of Robert Burns are buried here including Lord Monboddo and William Creech.

Greyfriars Kirk takes its name from the Franciscan Friary originally on this site. The kirkyard was founded in 1561 to take the place of St Giles' graveyard which was deemed to be full.

Following the defeat of the Covenanters at Bothwell Bridge in 1679, twelve hundred of the defeated army were kept prisoner in a field to the south of the kirkyard. This later became an area of vaulted tombs, and became known as the *Covenanters' Prison*.

In more recent times the graveyard was associated with Greyfriars Bobby, the loyal dog that slept on his master's grave for 13 years. Bobby's grave is situated at the entrance to the kirkyard in unconsecrated ground, and his master's grave lies on the eastern path.

Some with connections to Robert Burns who are buried here are: Allan Ramsay (poet), Henry MacKenzie (writer), William Creech (publisher), John Kay (caricaturist) and Henry and Harriet Siddons (Theatre Royal) who are buried to the left-hand side of the Covenanters' Prison.

James Burnett, Lord Monboddo, with his daughter Elizabeth, are buried together in the family crypt.

Some graves are in the vaulted tombs, which are situated in the Covenanters' Prison section. This is normally locked and at the moment access is via an organised kirkyard tour. Contact Greyfriars Kirk for more information.

Greyfriars Kirk
88 Candlemaker Row
Edinburgh
EH1 2QQ
0131 225 1900
administrator@greyfriarskirk.com
www.greyfriarskirk.com

The Kirk, shop and Greyfriars Museum are open to the general public between April and October.

Opening Times:
Monday–Friday 10.30–16.30
Saturday 11.00–14.00

Below: Harriet Siddons

Bottom: Henry Siddons

George Square

The area bounded by Bristo Street, Potterrow and College Street were all demolished and removed to make way for new university buildings and roads. The realigned Bristo Street has been renamed Chapel Street and Lothian Road. Bristo Place remains.

1 George Square

2 15 Buccleuch Place

3 Buccleuch Pend

4 Archers' Hall

5 Sciennes Hill House

6 50 Rankeillor Street

7 Nicolson Square and site of Alison Square

8 Potterrow (site of)

9 Buccleuch Parish Church

10 The Pear Tree

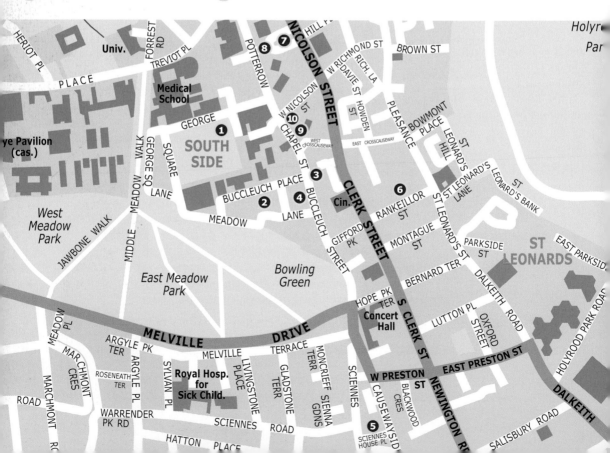

George Square
EH8 9LD

Burns' friend and patron, the Duchess of Gordon, lived here. At one time this square was also the home of Walter Scott.

Below: Walter Scott's House, George Square

George Square was designed in 1766 by the architect James Bow and very quickly became a popular place to stay. Housing in the Old Town had reached bursting point; it was overcrowded, unsanitary and riddled with disease and crime. These superior houses were soon bought by the richest of the city.

A list of residents reads like a who's who of the affluent and aristocratic. Admirals Duncan and Maitland, Lords Balgray, Dundas and Blair, Walter Scott, Lady Don, Countess of Glasgow and the high-profile Jane, Duchess of Gordon all quickly bought property here.

The Duchess of Gordon was a friend of Burns and a leading figure of the Caledonian Hunt Ball. When she met Robert Burns she was so taken with him that it was in her drawing room that Burns first read his poetry to Edinburgh society. Robert Burns would certainly have spent much time in this area.

There were riots in this quiet garden when in July 1767, in the Court of Session, Lord Dundas used his casting vote on the 'Douglas Cause' case. An angry mob stormed the square smashing the windows of the lawyers and judges involved. Rioting in the city lasted for 2 days.

Sadly many of these fine buildings were removed to make way for modern university buildings. The family home of Walter Scott was here at No. 25 where he stayed until he was married and moved to 108 George Street, 2nd Floor.

The Douglas Cause

Jane Douglas was the heir to the Douglas fortune so long as she did not die childless, in which case the fortune and titles would go to the Duchess of Hamilton.

Jane was unmarried until 1746 when she wed Colonel John Stewart. She was 48 at the time.

The couple went to the continent and, 2 years later, returned to Scotland with 'twin boys', Archibald and Sholto, who were said to have been born in Paris.

Jane and Sholto both died in 1753. In the care of the Duke of Queensberry, young Archibald changed his surname from Stewart to Douglas. He entered into an inheritance of £12,000 per year, an incredible sum at that time.

Unsurprisingly, the Hamiltons objected. They sent an investigator to Paris who returned with some surprising information: Archibald was actually Jacques Mignon who had been kidnapped in 1748 by *"a lady, a gentleman, and their maid"*; Sholto was the son of Sanry the Rope Dancer who had vanished in similar circumstances.

The investigator concluded that Jane's pregnancy was a complete fabrication.

In 1762, the Hamiltons raised an action at the Court of Session in Edinburgh. Their claim was that Archibald was not a Douglas, had no right to the inheritance, and that it was absurd to claim that Jane could have had twins at the age of 50.

The case lasted 8 years and proved a bonanza for the legal profession racking up costs of £52,000 [£5.2 million in today's values]. Eventually, the judges were split down the middle and the Lord President, Robert Dundas, had to use his casting vote: he came down in favour of the Hamiltons.

Archibald's lawyers immediately launched an appeal to the House of Lords in London, with many of the population betting on the outcome. The decision, after a month of debate, was unanimously reversed and Edinburgh went wild. Even during the hearing, a private detective had challenged to a duel one of Archibald's lawyers who had called him a liar – they both fired their pistols but both missed.

The judges who had opposed Douglas had their George Square windows smashed and the mob plundered the Hamilton apartments in Holyrood House. There was rioting throughout the city for 2 days, culminating in troops being called in to restore order.

In 1827, Archibald died as Baron Douglas of Douglas, aged 79. He was one of the richest landowners in the country.

In 2008, letters were found in the archives of the Earl of Home written by Archibald's mother, Jane, and one of her lawyers. They strongly indicate that she and her husband did actually buy the babies in Paris.

Above: (left) Archibald, 1st Lord Douglas, and (right) Lady Jane Douglas

Below: Holyrood Palace

Sir Walter Scott
1771–1832 Writer

George Square

Above: Sir Walter Scott

Walter Scott was born in College Wynd, Edinburgh on 15th August 1771. He was the 10th child of Walter Scott (1729–99) and Anne Rutherford (1739–1819).

His father was a successful solicitor and his grandfather Dr John Rutherford (1695–1779) was a professor of physiology in Edinburgh University.

In 1773, Scott contracted polio and was sent to his grandfather's farm in Roxburghshire where he was taught to read by his Aunt Jenny, hearing tales and legends that would later characterise his own work.

The illness left Walter lame in one leg and great efforts were made to cure this disability. By the time he was 7 he could walk well enough to attend the Royal High School of Edinburgh, becoming a prolific reader of a wide variety of books.

On finishing school he returned to his aunt in Kelso, attending the local grammar school, where he met James and John Ballantyne, with whom he later entered into partnership.

At the age of 12, in November 1783, Scott entered Edinburgh University, but left early, in 1786, without taking a degree, so that he could begin his training as a solicitor with his father. While at university Scott became a friend of Adam Ferguson, son of Professor Adam Ferguson who hosted literary salons. It was at these meetings that the young Scott met Thomas Blacklock, The Blind Poet, who also loaned him books.

In the winter of 1786–87 the 15-year-old Scott saw Burns at one of the salons in Sciennes Hill House. Burns noticed a print illustrating the poem, *The Justice of the Peace* and asked who had written the poem. Only the young Scott knew that it was by John Langhorne, and told Burns. This was to be their only meeting although Scott did see Burns in the street shortly after. Burns was looking through books in a stall and Scott tells that he was so in awe of the man that he was afraid to approach him.

In 1789 Scott returned to university to study moral philosophy under Dugald Stewart, also founding in the same year the Literary Society, which met for two years in the Masonic lodge in Carrubber's Close. Society members included Adam Ferguson, Joseph Black and James Hutton.

Scott did not formally graduate from university but instead, on the 6th July 1792, passed the Scots law examinations of the Faculty of Advocates.

While on a visit to the Lake District, Scott met Charlotte Genevieve Charpentier, a ward of Lord Downshire in Cumberland. Within 3 weeks Scott proposed and the couple were married in Carlisle on Christmas Eve 1797. He was engaged before he broke the news to his parents, or had told them anything about her, including that she was French.

In 1799 he was appointed Sheriff-Depute of the County of Selkirk. By this time Scott had taken his first steps into writing and this, along with his job and inheritances, meant that they had a comfortable lifestyle.

In 1796, Scott's childhood friend James Ballantyne had founded a printing press in Kelso and through Ballantyne, Scott was able to publish his first works. The books were a great success and in 1805, Scott invested and became a partner in the highly profitable printing business, John Ballantyne & Company. He wrote a succession of books to ensure continued growth of the company, and provided additional finance which was needed for expansion.

Scott's love of Scottish history, and his fascination for the country's legends,

led to Scott being given permission to search for the long-lost Scottish Crown Jewels which had been missing since the days of Oliver Cromwell and Charles II. In 1818 Scott and a small team unearthed the treasure from the depths of Edinburgh Castle. A grateful Prince Regent awarded Scott the title of Baronet; he was now known as Sir Walter Scott.

After George IV's accession to the throne, Scott convinced the king to visit Edinburgh and Scott was invited to stage-manage the visit. The pageant was spectacularly successful and Scott urged the the king to wear tartan, convincing him that the public would love him for it. George IV duly obliged, wearing pink tights under a bright red Stewart tartan. This event marked tartan as a potent symbol of Scottish identity.

Above: The Meeting of Robert Burns and Sir Walter Scott at Sciennes Hill House, by Charles Martin Hardie, 1893.

In the 1826 banking crisis the Ballantyne business crashed, leaving Scott, who had invested heavily, completely ruined. He refused to declare himself bankrupt, or borrow from friends, but instead put all of his assets into a trust for creditors and vowed to write his way clear of debt.

Scott worked tirelessly to pay off his creditors, writing introductions and notes for his novels which were published in a serial form of one a month between 1829 and 1833, selling in huge numbers and totalling 48 volumes.

He also undertook a European tour, but on his return to Scotland in 1830 he suffered a stroke. After a third stroke in April 1831, he died at Abbotsford on 21st September 1832, aged 61.

By the time he died he had reduced the debt by half. In 1833 Scott's family sold his copyrights and all the creditors were paid in full.

Memorials to Sir Walter Scott are to be found throughout Scotland. In Edinburgh, the Scott Monument, standing 200½ feet in height, was completed in Princes Street in 1844, and Edinburgh's Waverley Station takes its name from one of his novels. In Glasgow, the Walter Scott Monument dominates the city's George Square.

The Walter Scott Prize for Historical Fiction is awarded annually at Scott's historic home, Abbotsford House, and at £25,000 is one of the largest prizes in British literature.

In 2010, Abbotsford House itself was awarded a lottery grant of £4.8m as part of a £14.5m project to preserve the Melrose property. The garden opened to visitors in 2012 with the main house welcoming visitors in 2013.

Abbotsford
Melrose
Roxburghshire
TD6 9BQ
01896 752043
www.scottsabbotsford.co.uk

Right: Abbotsford House

Assembly Rooms
15 Buccleuch Place, EH8 9LN

For a time, the Assembly Rooms were the centre of the social world of Edinburgh and Burns attended parties here.

Dancing was a very important social grace in Edinburgh, and it was here where important people were seen and where a reputation could be made or broken. There were several Assembly Rooms as they were called, in the city, but none more important than the Assembly Rooms on the first floor of No. 15 Buccleuch Place.

Between this tenement and the next is a small lane – Buccleuch Place Lane. If you walk up this lane to the end and glance back, you will note that only this tenement has an extension jutting into the back green. This was the original Assembly Rooms, the scene of many a dance party, before the rooms moved location to George Street just after Burns' stay in Edinburgh.

Alexander Dalziel noticed Burns at one of the parties here some time before 25th January 1787: *"I saw him at an assembly t'other night. The Duchess of Gordon and other ladies of rank took notice of him there. He behaves wonderfully well; very independent in his sentiments, and has none of the mauvaise honte [bashfulness] about him, though he is not forward."*

Burns, with his gracious manners and wit, was a frequent and welcome guest at many of these gatherings and was befriended by the very beautiful Jane Maxwell, Duchess of Gordon herself, who was the society queen of Edinburgh. This friendship was genuine and important, and through her, doors opened to him, and many invitations to evening soirées fell his way.

Above: The Assembly Rooms, Buccleuch Place

Jane Maxwell Alexander, Duchess of Gordon

1748–1812 Patron and friend

15 Buccleuch Place

Above: The Duchess of Gordon

Sir Joshua Reynolds said that life in the Gordon Family was never dull, and Jane Maxwell, Duchess of Gordon lived life to the full.

As was usual with landowning families, a town house was rented and the Maxwell mother and three daughters resided for a time in Hurlford Close, midway along the Royal Mile, so that her girls could be well educated and become part of Edinburgh society. Jane was 11 years old when they moved.

As a child, Jane made a name for herself by riding on the back of a sow down the Royal Mile. (The pigs were let out for their daily exercise in the High Street). As a young girl, she somehow trapped a hand under the wheel, or in a door, of a carriage and had a finger torn off as it moved away. She had an ebony finger made and regularly wore a glove.

When she was 16, news reached her that the man she loved, thought to be Thomas Fraser, had been killed on the battlefield, and she agreed to marry the Duke of Gordon, thus ensuring the security of her family and, as Duchess of Gordon, attaining a high social position and much wealth.

However, while on honeymoon, she received a letter from the man supposed dead, announcing that he was well and was on the way home to marry her. It is reported that she fainted on reading the letter.

In Edinburgh, she met Robert Burns, and they formed a genuine friendship; the duchess subscribed to 21 copies of his *Edinburgh Edition*, while her patronage opened many doors and created opportunities for Burns. On his Highland Tour he had lunch with the duke and duchess and family in Gordon Castle, which Burns immortalised in his *Castle Gordon*.

The duchess had a hugely busy and entertaining life, so much so that it is not possible to list all of her achievements in this limited space.

She took over the finances of her husband's estate, increasing his wealth by £200,000, partly through fostering the art of weaving and increasing the range and colours of fabrics.

She was interested in the music of Scotland and was credited with establishing the Strathspey as a dance form.

When in London, as in Edinburgh, she was a leader of fashion and soon became a rival of Georgina, Duchess of Devonshire who was already established as a celebrated beauty and socialite. The Duchess of Gordon introduced tartan to London society, inventing a silk tartan material, which soon became a 'must have' accessory as far afield as Paris.

She did all this at a time when tartan was frowned upon in Scotland following the failed '45 Rebellion, but her friendship with George III and William Pitt made the silk tartan acceptable.

When in 1793 an army had to be assembled yet again, she went back to Scotland and toured villages and towns on a recruitment drive. Dressed in her self-designed uniform, with a tall hat and long black feather, would-be soldiers found they had to take the King's Shilling from between her lips by kissing her. She personally recruited almost 1,000 men and the Gordon Highlanders were formed.

Her marriage to the Duke of Gordon was not a happy one. It was a marriage in name only, for convenience and position in society. At almost the same time as the duchess gave birth to their first son and heir, the duke's mistress also gave birth to a son, both named George. *"My George, and the Duke's George"* was how she described the boys.

The duke installed his mistress at Gordon Castle while he had a small house built for the duchess, named Kinrara, on the banks of the River Spey where she stayed when in Scotland.

The duchess was well known for having secured good marriages, with suitable husbands, for all of her 4 daughters. When arranging a marriage partner for her fourth daughter, the potential husband's father, General Cornwallis, refused to approve the marriage citing alleged madness in the Gordon family. The duchess allayed his fears by swearing that *"there was not one drop of Gordon blood"* in the child. It is thought by some that the father was Thomas Fraser, her love who had returned from the dead.

The marriage was officially ended in 1805.

Below: Jane Maxwell, Duchess of Gordon by William Skeoch Cumming, 1897

Jane Maxwell, Duchess of Gordon, died on 14th April 1812, aged 64, her 4 daughters and surviving son by her side, in the Pulteney Hotel, Piccadilly, London.

The duchess's hearse was drawn all the way from London by 6 jet-black Belgian horses. When the cortege reached Dalwhinnie, the first stage within the Highland territory then belonging to the family, the body of the duchess lay in state for 2 days. It lay for a similar period at the inn at Pitmain, within half-a-mile of Kingussie, and was subsequently followed by an immense concourse of Highland people to the final resting place at her beloved Kinrara, in the Celtic Chapel by the banks of the Spey.

Castle Gordon

Below: The House on Kinrara Estate

Streams that glide in orient plains,
Never bound by Winter's chains;
Glowing here on golden sands,
There immixed with foulest stains
From Tyranny's empurpled hands:
These, their richly gleaming waves,
I leave to tyrants and their slaves;
Give me the stream that sweetly laves
The banks by Castle Gordon.

Spicy forests, ever gay,
Shading from the burning ray
Hapless wretches sold to toil;
Or the ruthless Native's way,
Bent on slaughter, blood, and spoil:
Woods that ever verdant wave,
I leave the tyrant and the slave;
Give me the groves that lofty brave
The storms, by Castle Gordon.

Wildly here without control,
Nature reigns and rules the whole;
In that sober, pensive mood,
Dearest to the feeling soul,
She plants the forest, pours the flood:
Life's poor day I'll musing rave,
And find at night a sheltering cave,
Where waters flow and wild woods wave
By bonie Castle Gordon.

Buccleuch Pend
27 Buccleuch Street, EH8 9LT

Burns stayed briefly here at the home of friend William Nicol who accompanied Burns on his tour of the Highlands.

A 'pend' is a passageway that passes through a building from a street to a courtyard.

The location of the Pend House is the gap between 15 and 27 Buccleuch Street. At one point around 23rd August 1787, Burns stayed in the top flat with William Nicol.

Burns never took to classical languages and found Nicol's flat rather noisy: *"Mr Nicol on the opposite side of the table takes to correct a proof-sheet of a thesis. – They are gabbling latin so loud that I cannot hear what my own soul is saying in my own scull …"*

William Nicol
1744–97 Teacher

Buccleuch Pend

Above: Buccleuch Pend in the 19th century

Below: William Nicol

Willie Nicol was born in Dumbretton, Annan in 1744. He studied for the ministry at Edinburgh University before switching to medicine and finally to Classics. In 1774 he was appointed Classics Master at the High School. He resigned in 1795 after a violent quarrel with Dr Adams, the rector, and, undeterred, opened his own school.

He taught Lord Cockburn who found him as a teacher *"someone who knew nothing of what it was to be young and who was incredibly strict"*. Words like vain, cantankerous, irascible, and pedant are often applied to him. Agnes McLehose did not like him at all. Walter Scott, also taught by him, described him thus: *"worthless, drunken, and inhumanly cruel to boys under his charge"*. It is reported that in revenge, Scott once pinned a paper to Nicol's coat-tail with a paragraph of the day's Latin lesson – altered by Scott to read *"Who is this worthless stranger who has approached our abode?"*

Robert Burns, on the other hand, found him *"honest hearted"*. Burns hated hypocrites and liked straight talking. He would certainly have found that quality in Nicol.

Nicol, as Scott said, liked a drink and Burns may have met him in a public house. While one biographer says they met at the Fencibles, yet another says that Nicol was not a welcome guest there. But on the ground floor of the tenement at

Buccleuch Pend there is said to have been Lucky Pringles Tavern.

Burns lodged with Nicol from 7th to 25th August 1787 and Nicol accompanied Burns on his tour of the Highlands in 1787. It was during this tour Burns chose to visit Castle Gordon alone, leaving Nicol at the village inn. Burns, reluctantly had to forego the opportunity to spend more time with the Duke and Duchess and their important friends, and had to rejoin the irate Nicol who threatened to continue on his own.

Burns never quite forgave Nicol for forcing him to leave the castle which is apparent in his *Epitaph for William Nicol*, but for all his faults, Burns liked Nicol and named a son after him: William Nicol Burns.

Above: Buccleuch Pend

In 1790 Nicol bought the small estate of Laggan in Dumfriesshire and 6 years later opened his own school.

Willie Nicol died on 21st April 1797, aged 53. He is buried in Old Calton Burial Ground, in an unmarked grave to the east of the Martyr's Obelisk.

It is reported that he had previously purchased 5 lairs, close to the Hume monument.

Nicol was married, with 7 children, three of whom survived him.

Epitaph For William Nicol

Ye maggots, feed on Nicol's brain,
For few sic feasts you've gotten;
And fix your claws in Nicol's heart,
For deil a bit o't's rotten.

Allan Masterton

c1750–99 Teacher

Buccleuch Pend

Masterton was a writing teacher in Stevenlaw's Close, (also known as Telfer's Close), off the High Street.

Burns met Masterton, through Willie Nicol, in Johnnie Dowie's Tavern in Liberton's Wynd and all 3 became great friends.

On a celebrated occasion they visited Nicol, either at his farm named Laggan in Nithsdale in the borders, or at Nicol's lodgings in Moffat. They celebrated into the night and the result was the famous drinking song *Willie Brew'd a Peck o' Mault* with music composed by Masterton. All 3 are named in the song.

Allan Masterton had a great knowledge of Scots songs and collaborated with Burns. One of their collaborations was *Beware o' Bonie Ann*, for Masterton's daughter Ann, with music composed by her father. This and several others are in the *Scots Musical Museum*.

Burns said of Masterton in a letter of October 1789, that he was *"… one of the worthiest men in the world"*.

Masterton was later to be a music teacher to Sir Walter Scott.

Allan Masterton died on 15th June 1799.

Below: Allan Masterton

Above: Johnnie Dowie

Left: Johnnie Dowie's Tavern

Archers' Hall
66 Buccleuch Street, EH8 9LR

The headquarters of The Royal Company of Scottish Archers, a select and aristocratic group. Robert Burns was admitted to their ranks in 1792.

Although it is recognised that The Royal Company of Archers, known as The Queen's Bodyguard in Scotland, have existed in some form for several hundred years, it wasn't until 1676 that the Company drew up Articles and Rules of Management with the body being recognised by The Privy Council on 6th March 1677. The Company was further granted a Royal Charter from Queen Anne on 31st December 1713.

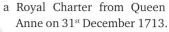

Today, members of the Company are chosen from those who are Scottish or who have a strong Scottish connection. Senior military officers, members of the nobility and politicians make up the majority of the current 530-strong membership. On 10th April 1792, Robert Burns was to become an Honorary Member.

Originally, Company members were selected from men of some high class who, in times of danger to the monarchy, attended the king as his chief bodyguard, distinguishing themselves for their loyalty, courage, and skill in archery.

Legend has it that in the bloody battlefield of Flodden in 1513, the body of James IV was found covered and surrounded by the bodies of his archers' guard.

Top: William St Clair

Above: Alexander Cunningham

Right, inset: Archers' Hall before the extension was built

In times of unrest it was important that all men over the age of 12 were proficient in archery. James IV, in 1491 decreed, *"in na place of the realme there be used fute-ball, golfe, or other unprofitable sports, for the common good of the realme and defense thereof, and that bowes and schutting be hanted"*(practiced). To this day The Royal Company of Archers champion the proficiency of archery in Scotland.

The Musselburgh Arrow, which is claimed as the oldest sporting trophy in the world, dating back to 1603, is competed for annually, the event taking place on Musselburgh Racecourse. From 1667, entry has been restricted to members of the Company.

Many of Burns' past and future connections were to be members: the Reverend

Left: Archers' Hall

Walker ('the Skating Minister'); Dr Nathaniel Spens, a member of the Royal College of Surgeons; Henry Scott, 1ˢᵗ Duke of Buccleuch, Governor of the Bank of Scotland; John Beugo, the engraver; Henry Erskine, Edinburgh lawyer; as was his friend Alexander Cunningham; William St Clair of Roslin, Grand Master Mason; Allan Ramsay the painter and Sir Walter Scott were only a few of the most eminent persons in Scotland whose company Burns was to join.

The members list from 1714 onward is copied from a parchment roll which each member has to sign, in his own hand. Robert Burns was never in Edinburgh after 1792 to personally sign the roll, but he did receive his diploma when in Dumfries and The Royal Company of Archers confirm there is no doubt that he was admitted as a member.

Burns' son, Lieutenant-Colonel James Glencairn Burns carried the diploma during his service in India and Colonel William Nicol Burns confirmed that the Indian heat may have destroyed the original seal. In 1862 Burns' sons presented the diploma to the collection being raised for the Edinburgh Burns Monument. Today the diploma can be viewed in the Writers Museum.

Top: Sir Adam Ferguson

Above: Dr Nathaniel Spens

Left: Henry Scott

Left, inset: The crest of The Royal Company of Archers

Sciennes Hill House
5 Sciennes House Place, EH9 1NW

In this house Robert Burns met a 15-year-old Walter Scott at a gathering of some of the greatest thinkers, scientists and academics to grace the city.

The word Sciennes is pronounced 'sheens'; the name being derived from that of a monastery dedicated to St Catherine of Sienna. In Burns' time, this area was a country village of weavers, called Sciennes.

The painting in the Writers' Museum *Robert Burns in James Sibbald's Circulating Library in Parliament Square Edin.* by William Borthwick Johnstone dates from 1856; the incident it purports to illustrate – the day Walter Scott, the future novelist, met Robert Burns – is pure fiction, as are so many 'historical' paintings of Burns.

The place where a young Walter Scott actually did meet Burns is here at Sciennes Hill House and our authority for this is not only Walter Scott himself in a letter he wrote to John G. Lockhart in 1827, but also Adam Ferguson, the son of Professor Adam Ferguson whose house this was.

Walter Scott was only 15 in 1787, but was already a clerk in his father's law office. He had been invited to Sciennes Hill House along with Dr Dugald Stewart, Joseph Black, the scientist, James Hutton, the geologist and John Home, the author of *Douglas*.

Dr Dugald Stewart was acquainted with Burns and offered to bring him along, an idea to which the professor readily agreed. At first Burns seemed shy in the illustrious company and wandered around the room looking at the professor's collection of pictures. Burns then stopped in front of a picture by William Henry Bunbury (1750–1811), artist and caricaturist.

Burns was visibly moved by the depiction of a soldier lying dead in the snow. There were

Top: Adam Ferguson

Above: James Hutton

Right: Sciennes Hill House

lines written below the painting and Burns, moved to tears by them, asked who had written them. Scott was too shy to speak directly to Burns, but according to Sir Adam Ferguson, it was to his son, also Adam, to whom Scott whispered that the lines came from a poem by John Langhorne, *The Justice of the Peace*. Scott's friend gave this answer to Burns who was very much impressed and he briefly addressed young Scott. According to young Adam the words of Burns to Scott were: *"You'll be a man yet, sir."*

Left: The commemorative plaques from the rear wall of Sciennes House. According to the note on the smaller plaque it is possible to view the north front between the hours of 2pm and 5pm, access being via No. 7 Hill House Place.

Below: Joseph Black

Rankeillor Street
EH8 9HZ

Around 1858, in a house here, dozens of Burns manuscripts were used as drawing paper for children to pass their time.

Dr Alexander Maxwell Adams was a doctor in Edinburgh's south side. His practice was at 26 St Patrick Square. His son, James, played as a boy with Duff Findlater who lived in Rankeillor Street.

Duff's mother, Mrs Mary Hewen was the widow of James Findlater, who was the eldest son of Alexander Findlater, Burns' supervisor and friend in the Excise in Dumfries.

James Adams recalls that he visited the house regularly and that Mrs Findlater had a large number of Burns' writings. They lay on a large table desk freely available to the boys. He describes the paper as *"Stiff and rough on surface, usually with one or more ragged edges, as if from a half-sheet being torn or cut across or as if dragged out of a book, which was indeed the case, as we were told they had been taken from old Excise ledgers. We frequently used the unwritten-upon sides of the sheets for drawing houses, beasts and boats ..."*

Dr Adams later acquired many of the manuscripts from Mrs Findlater.

Below: Rankeillor Street

Adams reports that even at a young age, when playing with the Burns papers, he could recognise the distinctive handwriting, because he regularly saw and handled papers like it at his own home!

Jean Lorimer, was also one of his father's patients but, as she was not *"very well off"* his father declined to make any charge. In return for his professional services, Jean apparently gave Dr Adams the Burns papers *"in grateful acknowledgement of his professional services"*. James Adams writes that while still a schoolboy he made the short journey on more than one occasion to her home in Middleton Entry to collect a packet of Burns' manuscripts.

The Post Office directory of 1846–47 for Edinburgh and Leith, lists Mrs Findlater as residing at No. 50 Rankeillor St.

Alexander Findlater
1754–1839 Collector of Excise

Rankeillor Street

Alexander Findlater, was a Collector of Excise in Glasgow and was promoted to become Supervisor in Dumfries in April 1791.

Findlater had recommended Burns in 1789, when Burns applied for a position in the Excise and Burns subsequently wrote in thanks for the character reference that Findlater had provided.

The two were friends, exchanging letters on a regular basis, but the friendship did not prevent Findlater reprimanding Burns when required over excise matters and in a letter Burns apologises profusely for an apparent lack of scrutiny in an inspection saying, "*I have not surveyed there since his return. I know the gentleman's ways are, like the grace of G—, past all comprehension; but I shall give the house a severe scrutiny tomorrow morning, and send you in the naked facts … and as the gentleman is known to be an illicit Dealer, and particularly as this is the single instance of the least shadow of carelessness or impropriety in my conduct as an Officer, I shall be peculiarly unfortunate if my character shall fall a sacrifice to the dark manoeuvres of a Smuggler.*"

In 1792 Findlater defended Burns at an excise inquiry when charges of disloyalty were raised against him. Burns was cleared of any wrongdoing.

These incidents didn't affect Burns' standing and he was made Acting Supervisor in 1794 when Findlater became ill.

In Burns' final days Findlater was a regular visitor. On the poet's final evening on earth Findlater tried to entice Burns to eat and attempted to provide some comfort to the dying man.

After Burns' death, Findlater defended Burns' habits when biographers Currie and Heron sought to brand Burns as a "*hopeless drunkard*".

Findlater worked in Glasgow from 1811 until his retirement in 1825. The Burns Society erected a memorial to him in North Street Burial Ground in Glasgow.

Above: Alexander Duff Findlater

Nicolson Square
Formerly the site of Alison Square

An invitation to tea in Alison Square was one of the most important meetings of Burns' life.

Alison Square, was removed in the clearance and regeneration of the houses and roads around the Potterrow, Bristo Street and Nicolson Square area. By the removal of the centre row of tenements between Nicolson and Alison Squares, a larger Nicolson Square was created (formerly spelled Nicholson's).

Miss Erskine Ebenezer Nimmo lived in a first-floor apartment in Alison Square, keeping house for her nephew, William Nimmo, a supervisor in the Excise at Lanark. Although Burns was later to work for the Excise, his connection with Miss Nimmo was most likely through their mutual friendship with Margaret Chalmers.

On the afternoon of 4th December 1787, Miss Nimmo gave a tea party to which she invited Burns.

Another friend of Miss Nimmo – Agnes Craig McLehose – had read the *Edinburgh Edition* of Burns and was keen to meet this talented writer, but her cousin William Craig, later to become Lord Craig, did not approve of him. Agnes was mindful of the assistance and help that Craig had given her in her troubles with her husband and his subsequent support.

Like her cousin, Agnes read a lot, liked conversation, and wrote poetry. But William Craig refused to invite "*that ploughman with pretensions to poetry*" to any of his soirées. So, Agnes contrived to be invited to Miss Nimmo's on the occasion which Burns attended and this meeting changed both their lives forever.

Burns refers to Miss Nimmo "*in her usual pleasant way*" rallying him [poking mild fun at him] a good deal on his new acquaintance and following the meeting Burns sent Agnes a poem because Miss Nimmo told him Agnes is "*not only a Critic but a Poetess*".

Below: Site of Alison Square

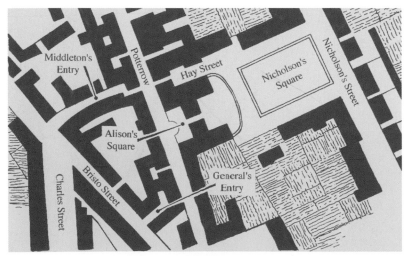

Patrick Miller of Dalswinton

1731–1815 Banker, inventor, landlord

18 Nicolson Square, EH8 9BH

Patrick Miller was a merchant seaman in his early life before becoming a banker in Edinburgh. He was made a director of the Bank of Scotland in 1767, later becoming deputy chairman. He was also a shareholder in the Carron Company engineering works and had a great interest in naval architecture which led him to try to interest European navies in his designs.

He engaged William Symington, a mechanical engineer at Wanlockhead lead mines, to build his design of a twin-hulled pleasure boat which was successfully tested on Dalswinton Loch, Dumfriesshire, near his home on 14th October 1788.

In December 1788, Miller converted a canal boat by adding a steam engine – from a plan by Symington – which tugged a heavy load on the Forth and Clyde Canal at a speed of 7 miles an hour. However, Miller suddenly abandoned the project having become satisfied that the steam engine, as designed, was not practical. Symington however was to continue with his work and, using an engine designed by James Watt, produced in 1801, the world's first practical steamboat, the *Charlotte Dundas*.

Above: Patrick Miller

Below: Mrs Patrick Miller

Left: Patrick Miller's Steam Boat on Dalswinton Loch, 1788

Burns discovered that it had been Patick Miller who was *"the anonymous hand"* who had left 10 guineas for him with James Sibbald when Burns had only been in Edinburgh for 2 weeks, a philanthropic gesture from a wealthy man to a genius.

Sibbald, was a publisher and bookseller in Edinburgh, and was the first to carry a review of the *Kilmarnock Edition* of Burns' poems. He went on to publish extracts of Burns' poetry, alongside very favourable reviews. Burns' was deeply grateful and sent a letter of thanks to Sibbald in January 1787. Burns writes, *"The warmth with which you have befriended an obscure man and young author, in your three last magazines – I can only say, Sir, I feel the weight of the obligation, and wish I could express my sense of it. – In the meantime, accept this conscious acknowledgement …"* The letter can be viewed in the Robert Burns Birthplace Museum in Alloway.

Burns met Patrick Miller shortly afterwards and the two became friends.

Miller owned the Dalswinton Estate near Dumfries, and Burns was to eventually rent the Ellisland Farm from him. The farm was a failure for many reasons and the relationship soured while Burns tried to find a way out of the lease.

Once the problem of the lease was solved the pair became friendly once more.

Williamson's Directory of 1786 lists a Peter Miller of Dalswinton at No. 18 Nicolson Square

Patrick Miller died at Dalswinton on 9th December 1815, aged 84. His remains are buried in Greyfriars Kirkyard.

Right: Nicolson Square

General's Entry
Potterrow, near EH8 9BT

Agnes McLehose lived here as a plaque nearby reminds us. Burns visited her here and sent many letters to her at this address.

A plaque on the corner of Potterrow at the junction with Nicolson Square is all that indicates to us that, when Burns was in Edinburgh in 1787–88, Agnes McLehose lived nearby in the now demolished General's Entry.

Below: Agnes McLehose (Clarinda)'s House, exterior

General's Entry is named after General George Monk, one of Oliver Cromwell's trusted generals who, according to tradition, had his mansion here. This in unlikely to be true as he resided with his family in Dalkieth House. He would, however, have been a regular visitor.

When Cromwell entered Scotland in 1650, he defeated and subjugated the entire country before pursuing Charles II in England, leaving General Monk to rule over Scotland. Monk's rule was ruthless resulting in poverty and starvation nationwide, only ending in 1659 when he marched his army from Coldstream to a London which had descended into chaos and anarchy after the death of Cromwell, a move which restored Charles II and the monarchy.

Agnes rented a small flat on the first floor of a tenement in a close at the back of General's Entry.

It is a short walk from here to St James Square where Burns was living; a walk that both Agnes and Burns made often.

Agnes brought up 3 children here, receiving no money or assistance from her estranged husband, managing to get by with small annuities and support from her cousin Lord William Craig.

About 1810 Agnes moved to a more comfortable house in Calton Hill.

Above: A plaque marks the site of Clarinda's House

Left inset: Clarinda's House, interior

Robert Ainslie
1766–1838 Businessman and friend
Potterrow

Robert Ainslie was born on the 13th January 1766 in Berrywell, into a very respected family in Duns, in the Scottish Borders, his father being the factor of Lord Douglas's Estates at Berrywell.

Above: Robert Ainslie

Ainslie was a law student in Samuel Mitchelson's law office in Edinburgh when Burns first met him in 1787. He was 7 years older than Burns, but, sharing a love of song, good living and, of course women, it was inevitable that they should meet and become very good friends.

He joined Burns on the first leg of his tour of the Borders in May 1787 and they enjoyed each other's company. Said Burns: "*I have not a friend upon earth besides yourself, to whom I can talk nonsense without forfeiting some degree of his esteem.*"

At Eyemouth, on the east coast, when both were made Royal Arch Masons of the local Masonic lodge, Ainslie was charged the fee of 1 guinea, while Burns was admitted 'gratis'.

Burns trusted Ainslie and he became the recipient of several of Burns' most famous letters, being a confidant as well as a friend. Burns also told him of his relationship with Agnes, taking him along to visit Agnes at Potterrow.

Ainslie married Jane Cunningham in 1798.

In his later years Ainslie lost the carefree attitude of his youth and developed a serious and formidable reputation in the business world, dividing his time between his Hill Street office in Edinburgh and his estate at Edingham near Dalbeattie.

He wrote several papers on agricultural subjects and the legal and financial matters as they affected landowners.

Burns would have been shocked to find his former carousing partner turning to God and religion in his later years when he became an elder of the Kirk, writing many homilies and religious works including *A Father's Gift to his Children* and *Reasons for Hope In Us.*

Ainslie died in 1838, aged 72 and is buried in Duns Churchyard where a fine monument survives.

Reverend John Kemp
1745–1805 Churchman

Potterrow

The biographer James Mackay describes the Reverend Kemp as a *"sanctimonious lecher"*. He exerted a great influence over the very religious Agnes McLehose with his sermons, but was not himself a very good man.

In 1776 he was called to the New Greyfriars Church and then in 1779 to the Tolbooth Church.

Kemp resided for several years in Ramsay Garden, subsequently moving to the Netherbow, now the site of The Scottish Storytelling Centre on The Royal Mile.

He had three wives and an affair with Lady Colquhoun of Luss with only his death saving him from scandal and ruin. In other words, he was a hypocritical Holy Willie, the very kind of churchman that Burns despised and ridiculed in *Holy Willie's Prayer*, but Agnes, blinded by religious fervour and his 'hellfire' sermons did not see him this way.

Holy Willie's Prayer is a poem which Burns wrote in 1785 about an elder, Willie Fisher, in the parish church of Mauchline, Ayrshire. It was printed anonymously as a pamphlet in 1789 and is one of the finest satires ever written as an attack on the bigotry and hypocrisy of some members of the Kirk.

Fisher snooped and spied on folk and reported their wrongdoing to the church minister whilst he himself was a sinner and a hypocrite.

He provoked the Kirk Session to take action against Gavin Hamilton, a landlord and treasurer of the church, who was accused of financial impropriety and for failing to observe the sabbath. The accusations were heard and adjudicated by the presbytery of Ayr, a council of ministers and elders. Hamilton won the case.

Above: Dr John Kemp

Below: Gavin Hamilton

The name 'Holy Willie' has become integrated into the Scots language, describing a person who is humourless and hypocritically pious.

After Kemp's last wife died in 1801, he became 'close' to Lady Colquhoun, whose daughter had married Kemp's son David.

Sir James, 24th of Colquhoun and 26th of Luss, Sheriff Depute of Dumbartonshire, to give him his full title, took an action for divorce on the grounds of her association with Reverend Kemp.

Enormous scandal to all was averted in April 1805 when Sir James and Reverend Kemp both died with days of each other. Reverend Kemp died of a stroke on the 18th at Weirbank House near Melrose, while Sir James died on the 23rd in Edinburgh.

Address to the Unco Guid

O ye wha are sae guid yoursel',
Sae pious and sae holy,
Ye've nought to do but mark and tell
Your neibours' fauts and folly!
Whase life is like a weel-gaun mill,
Supplied wi' store o' water;
The heaped happer's ebbing still,
An' still the clap plays clatter.

Hear me, ye venerable core,
As counsel for poor mortals
That frequent pass douce Wisdom's door
For glaikit Folly's portals:
I, for their thoughtless, careless sakes,
Would here propone defences
Their donsie tricks, their black mistakes,
Their failings and mischances.

Ye see your state wi' theirs compared,
And shudder at the niffer;
But cast a moment's fair regard,
What maks the mighty differ;
Discount what scant occasion gave,
That purity ye pride in;
And (what's aft mair than a' the lave),
Your better art o' hidin.

Think, when your castigated pulse
Gies now and then a wallop!
What ragings must his veins convulse,
That still eternal gallop!
Wi' wind and tide fair i' your tail,
Right on ye scud your sea-way;
But in the teeth o' baith to sail,
It maks a unco lee-way.

See Social Life and Glee sit down,
All joyous and unthinking,
Till, quite transmugrified, they're grown
Debauchery and Drinking:
O would they stay to calculate
Th' eternal consequences;
Or your more dreaded hell to state,
Damnation of expenses!

Ye high, exalted, virtuous dames,
Tied up in godly laces,
Before ye gie poor Frailty names,
Suppose a change o' cases;
A dear-lov'd lad, convenience snug,
A treach'rous inclination
But let me whisper i' your lug,
Ye're aiblins nae temptation.

Then gently scan your brother man,
Still gentler sister woman;
Tho' they may gang a kennin wrang,
To step aside is human:
One point must still be greatly dark,
The moving Why they do it;
And just as lamely can ye mark,
How far perhaps they rue it.

Who made the heart, 'tis He alone
Decidedly can try us;
He knows each chord, its various tone,
Each spring, its various bias:
Then at the balance let's be mute,
We never can adjust it;
What's done we partly may compute,
But know not what's resisted.

Jenny Clow

1768–1792 Maid to Agnes McLehose, mother to Robert Burns Clow

Potterrow

Jenny Clow was born in Newburgh, Fife in 1768, the youngest of a family of 8. For some time she was Agnes McLehose's maid.

Friday 25th January 1788, was Robert Burns' 29th birthday. Far from being in a celebratory mood, he was stuck in the attic flat in St James Square, recovering from a damaged knee and had settled into a bout of depression.

Perhaps to avoid the possibility of gossip that might have come with the constant to and fro of the Penny Post, Agnes sent Jenny with a letter. Jenny then went on a errand to Leith and returned later to collect Burns' reply.

Either on this very occasion (or very shortly afterwards) Burns had 'relations' with the 20 year old. After all it was his birthday, and he was unable to see Agnes that day.

In November Jenny gave birth to a son she named Robert Burns, it being the custom of the time for children born out of wedlock to adopt the father's name.

Robert Burns Clow moved to England and became a rich merchant. His son, also Robert Burns Clow, was born in or around 1820. He became a trader in the East Indies and was killed by pirates in September 1851.

It is very likely that Burns had met Jenny before, since he had by then visited Agnes' house 5 times, and perhaps this was why she was entrusted with the letter. Agnes could not have foreseen the consequences.

Robert Ainslie informed Burns of Jenny's pregnancy and Burns sent her some money also offering to have the child brought up as his own but Jenny was adamant that the boy, Robert Burns Clow, remained with her.

In November 1791, Agnes wrote to Burns in Ayrshire; Jenny was dying. She had left Agnes' service and was living in straightened circumstances.

Burns took leave from his excise duties and travelled to Edinburgh, seeking out the by now very ill Jenny. He gave her a sum of money, but again Jenny refused to allow him to take the boy.

In January 1792, Jenny died of tuberculosis, aged 24.

John Miers

1756–1821 Artist

Potterrow

His career began in Leeds where he took over his father's business as a coach-painter and gilder. John Miers became a famous producer of shades – a profilist or silhouettist. Prior to this the only way of capturing a likeness was for an artist to carry out a portrait of the subject. Creating a shade was a much quicker and far less expensive process, only losing popularity when photography became more affordable around 1855.

Shades, or silhouettes as they later became known, were often made into breastpins, lockets or other jewellery. Burns gave many of these beloved images as presents to his friends.

Miers worked in Leeds from 1781 until 1785. As his shades became the most successful part of his business Miers and his family travelled around the country capitalising on their popularity, spending 2 years, 1786 and 1787, in Edinburgh, followed by 7 weeks in Glasgow before moving to London.

Using a candle to project a shadow of his subject onto a sheet of oiled paper, Miers then carefully traced the outline. He made reduced outlines from this original and filled them with black ink. Miers kept duplicates and had upwards of 10,000 portraits of royalty, statesmen and celebrities, resulting in a collection of almost every man and woman of note of that time.

Miers' advertising stated: *"Perfect likenesses in miniature profile – with the most exact symmetry and animated expression of the features."* Burns agreed with him and arranged with Agnes that she should sit for a profile. The Scottish National Portrait Gallery has a Miers silhouette of Agnes McLehose on display.

In a letter to Robert Ainslie from Mauchline on 23rd June 1788 Burns writes, *"… Mr Miers, profile painter in your town, has executed a profile of Dr Blacklock for me; do me the favour to call for it, and sit to him yourself for me, which puts you in the same size as the Doctor's. The account of both profiles will be fifteen shillings, … You must not, my friend, refuse to sit. The time is short: when I sat to Mr Miers, I am sure he did not exceed two minutes. I propose hanging Lord Glencairn, The Doctor, and you in trio, over my new chimney-piece that is to be. Adieu!"*

Above: John Miers

In 1788 Miers opened studios at 162 The Strand, London, moving to No. 111 in 1791, where he remained for the rest his life. In the 1790s John Field was apprenticed to Miers.

Miers died *"after many months of illness"* on 2nd June 1821, in his 64th year. The business was willed equally to John Field and Miers' son William.

Craufurd Tait
1765–1832 Writer (Lawyer)
Potterrow

Another notable customer of John Miers in Edinburgh was Craufurd Tait, a Writer to the Signet of Edinburgh and friend of Robert Burns.

Craufurd's father, John Tait was the Laird of Harviestoun in Tillicoultry, Clackmannanshire, and entertained Burns there in the summer of 1787.

It was at Harviestoun that Burns met Margaret Chalmers, and Charlotte Hamilton, whom Burns described as *"The Fairest Maid on Devon Banks."* Charlotte was the half-sister of his friend Gavin Hamilton, and she later went on to marry Dr James Adair, Burns' travelling companion on his Stirlingshire tour.

When Craufurd inherited Harviestoun on his father's death in 1800 he set about remodelling it, building a castle, model farm, coach house and walled garden.

Craufurd married a daughter of the Lord President of The Court of Session, and Lord Justice General, Sir Ilay Campbell and their eldest son Archibald went on to become the Archbishop of Canterbury from 1869 till his death in 1882.

Sir Ilay Campbell himself won renown in the 'Douglas Cause' case (see p.158), pleading the appeal of Archibald Douglas to the House of Lords and was first to bring the news to Edinburgh. His carriage progressed in triumph up the High Street to his father's house where he greeted the following crowds with a cry of *"Douglas for ever!"*

Harviestoun Castle was demolished in the 1970s, but a nearby cairn marks the spot to commemorate Burns' visit.

Craufurd Tait died in 1832, aged 67, and is buried in the family mausoleum known as Tait's Tomb which lies midway between the villages of Dollar and Tillicoutry.

Above: Craufurd Tait

Buccleuch Parish Church
33 Chapel Street, EH8 9AY

The burial place of Dr Blacklock and Alison Cockburn Rutherfurd, is also said to be the burial place of William 'Deacon' Brodie after his public hanging at the Tolbooth on 1st October 1788, "*between layers 21 and 23*". The cemetery has been much neglected for years and his grave is unmarked.

On the outside wall of Buccleuch church, opposite West Nicolson Street, is a plaque to Alison Cockburn, whose grave is directly on the other side of the wall. Alison Cockburn seems to have met Robert Burns at Lord Monboddo's house.

Burns' poem *I Dreamed I Lay,* written c1776 when Burns was only 17, was influenced by her poem *The Flowers of the Forest*. Jean Lorimer, who is buried in the nearby East Preston Street Cemetery, references Alison Cockburn's poem in her own poem, *Floo'ers o' the Forest*.

Dr Blacklock, The Blind Poet, who inspired Burns to come to Edinburgh, is buried against the opposite wall.

Below: Buccleuch Church graveyard

Alison Cockburn Rutherfurd

1712–94 Poet

Chapel Street

Alison Cockburn was born in Selkirk on 8th October 1712, the daughter of Robert Rutherfurd, and for 60 years was one of the 'queens of Edinburgh Society' and author of *Floo'ers o' the Forest*.

In a letter in December 1786 she gave her opinion of Burns; *"The town is at present agog with the ploughman poet, who receives adulation with native dignity, and is the figure of profession, strong and coarse, but a most enthusiastic heart of LOVE. He has seen Duchess of Gordon and all the gay world. His favourite for looks and manners is Bess Burnet,* [sic] *no bad judge indeed!"*

She also said, *"The man will be spoiled if he can spoil, but he keeps with his simple manners and is quite sober."*

In July 1793, Burns wrote of her to his friend George Thomson, *" 'The Flowers of the Forest' is charming as a poem, and should be, and must be, set to notes; but, though out of your rule, the three stanzas beginning 'I've seen the smiling o' fortune beguiling,' are worthy of a place, were it but to immortalise the author of them, who is an old lady of my acquaintance, and at this moment living in Edinburgh."*

Above: Alison Cockburn Rutherfurd

Alison married an impoverished advocate, Patrick Cockburn, in 1731 and was forced to live for 4 years with an elderly father-in-law, *"an old Presbyterian of the deepest dye"*, who condemned cards, plays and dancing as ungodly.

She had a desperately sad life. Her mother died when she was 10 years old, and being the youngest of the family by 7 years she admits to being *"caressed in childhood"* and *"indulged in youth"*. As she grew older she lived through the sudden deaths of several members of her family before she nursed her husband through a long and painful stomach illness until he passed away in 1753.

Below: Alison Cockburn Rutherfurd's grave

A nephew came to stay with her; however he suffered from depression and shot himself twice in the head. The lead balls didn't penetrate deeply enough to kill him and after removing the lead balls Alison nursed him back to health, telling no one of the incident, and keeping everyone away for 40 days using the excuse of a fever. Tragically, a year after this attempt, the nephew did exactly the same thing, this time with much success.

Alison became ill. Her son, Captain Adam Cockburn was in Edinburgh at this time with his regiment and came to her help, taking her to stay with relatives until she was strong enough to return to Edinburgh. Shortly after her return, Captain Adam began to suffer a series of stomach complaints subsequently forcing him to resign his commission. Alison again found herself nursing a loved one and after a long and agonising illness her son died in 1780, aged 48.

Alison lived in Bristo Street, moving later to Crichton Street where she continued to meet and mix with the very highest of artistic circles.

Alison Cockburn died on 22nd November 1794, aged 82 and is buried in the kirkyard of Buccleuch Parish Church.

Dr Thomas Blacklock

1721–91 Minister, musician, poet

Pear Tree House, (West Nicolson House) 38 West Nicolson Street, EH8 9DD

On the upper floor of this house lived Dr Thomas Blacklock. It was his invitation to visit Edinburgh that led to Burns living in this city for the most important months of his life.

Thomas Blacklock was born in Annan on 10th November 1721. He was blinded by smallpox before he was 2 years old. Nevertheless, he achieved his ambition to study divinity at Edinburgh and obtained a post as a minister in Kirkudbright in 1762.

He tried his best there for 2 years, but his parishioners complained that he could not carry out all the duties required of his ministry because of his blindness. So it was, that in 1765, he was granted a small annuity by the church and moved to Edinburgh where he settled in the upper two floors of the house on Chapel Street. Originally known as Nicolson House, Pear Tree House as a building, now The Peartree Pub itself, The Counting House and the next-door pub The Blind Poet. The original title deeds required *"the planting of trees for the ornamentation of the city"*. Pear trees were grown on the side of the house and facing what is now a beer garden and outside stage.

Over the years Blacklock entertained prominent guests here including Samuel Johnson during his Edinburgh visit of 1773, and James Boswell, his companion and biographer. Blacklock also knew Benjamin Franklin, who has been featured on the $100 bill, one of the founding fathers of the United States.

Blacklock tutored, composed music, wrote poems; in short, he became one of the most important figures in Edinburgh. The walls of the pub currently next door to The Peartree, called The Blind Poet after Blacklock, are decorated with extracts from some of the great man's poems.

As soon as the *Kilmarnock Edition* of Burns' poems was published the Reverend George Lawrie of Loudoun parish near Mossgiel, sent a copy to Blacklock who

Above: Dr Blacklock

replied on 4th September 1786 with copious praise for the work and with a suggestion that a second and larger edition be published. Burns was shown Blacklock's letter about a fortnight later and almost at once dropped all other plans and headed for Edinburgh.

Burns and Blacklock finally met sometime before 5th February 1787. Burns wrote in a letter that the two *"meet very often"*.

Blacklock, naturally, needed people to read to him; Professor Dugald Stewart read him Burns' poems, but the most important of Blacklock's assistants in Burns' lifetime was Margaret (Peggy) Chalmers.

Dr Thomas Blacklock died at home in Chapel Street, Edinburgh on 7th July 1791 and is buried in the kirkyard of Buccleuch Parish Church nearby.

The Peartree & Counting House
38/6 West Nicolson Street
Edinburgh
EH8 9DD
0131 667 7533
info@counting-house.co.uk
www.counting-house.co.uk

Left: Pear Tree House

As the building dates from the mid-1700s, and accesses throughout are by staircases, there is no wheelchair access to the Counting House, Blind Poet and Peartree, the premises which make up Pear Tree House.

Epistle to Dr Blacklock

Wow, but your letter made me vauntie!
And are ye hale, and weel, and cantie?
I kend it still your wee bit jauntie
Wad bring ye to:
Lord send you ay as weel's I want ye,
And then ye'll do.

The Ill-thief blaw the Heron south!
And never drink be near his drouth!
He tald myself, by word o' mouth,
He'd tak my letter;
I lippen'd to the chiel in trouth,
And bade nae better.

But aiblins honest Master Heron
Had at the time, some dainty Fair One,
To ware this theologic care on,
And holy study;
And tired o' sauls to waste his lear on,
E'en tried the body.

But what d'ye think, my trusty Fier,
I'm turn'd a Gauger – Peace be here!
Parnassian Quines I fear, I fear,
Ye'll now disdain me,
And then my fifty pounds a year
Will little gain me.

Ye glaiket, gleesome, dainty Damies,
Wha by Castalia's wimplin streamies,
Lowp, sing, and lave your pretty limbies,
Ye ken, ye ken,
That strang Necessity supreme is
'Mang sons o' Men.

I hae a wife and twa wee laddies,
They maun hae brose and brats o' duddies;
Ye ken yoursels my heart right proud is,
I need na vaunt;
But I'll sned bosoms and thraw saught-woodies
Before they want.

Lord help me thro' this warld o' care!
I'm weary sick o't late and air!
Not but I hae a richer share
Than mony ithers;
But why should ae man better fare,
And a' Men brithers!

Come, Firm Resolve, take thou the van,
Thou stalk o' carl-hemp in man!
And let us mind, faint heart ne'er wan
A lady fair:
Wha does the utmost that he can,
Will whyles do mair.

But to conclude my silly rhyme
(I'm scant o' verse and scant o' time),
To make a happy fireside clime
To weans and wife,
That's the true Pathos and Sublime
Of Human life.

My Compliments to Sister Beckie,
And eke the same to honest Lucky;
I wat she is a daintie Chuckie,
As e'er tread clay!
And gratefully, my gude auld Cockie,
I'm yours for ay.

Margaret Chalmers
1763–1843 Friend

The Pear Tree House, West Nicolson Street

Margaret was born in Fingland, Kirkcudbrightshire in 1763. Sometime later the family moved to Mauchline where it is likely that Burns and Margaret first met.

She sang and played the piano, and with her knowledge of literature and art it is no surprise at all that Burns fell in love with her. Margaret was friendly with the poet Thomas Campbell. Many years later when she was a widow Margaret told Campbell that Burns had proposed to her in October 1787, but she was engaged at the time to Lewis Hay. Despite her rejection of his marriage proposal, Burns remained friendly with the couple, writing numerous letters to Margaret over a long period.

Burns wrote two songs for her, *My Peggy's Face* and *When Braving Angry Winter's Storms*. Burns was surprised when Margaret rejected *My Peggy's Face*. She was secretly engaged to Lewis Hay at the time and knew that she would have been recognised and embarrassed by their publication.

While *When Braving Angry Winter's Storms* appeared in the second volume of the *Scots Musical Museum*, *My Peggy's Face* didn't appear in print until 1802, long after Burns' death.

Above: Margaret Chalmers

In 1788 Margaret did marry Lewis Hay, a banker and a partner in Forbes, Hunter, and Co. The married couple then moved to a company property in Parliament Square in Edinburgh.

When she was in Edinburgh, she often played the piano and sang for Dr Blacklock. It is very likely that at Blacklock's home in West Nicholson Street, Burns would have met her again.

Burns in fact told Agnes McLehose that he held Margaret in the same esteem as he did her. Typically of Burns, his correspondence with the two women was being conducted at the same time.

The Hays had 3 daughters and 3 sons and moved to the continent where Lewis died in February 1800. Margaret then returned to Edinburgh, residing at No. 12 Buccleuch Place. Around 1820 she again moved abroad and died in 1843, aged 80, in Pau in the Pyrenees.

Part of Margaret's obituary in *The London Standard* on 4th April 1843 reads:

DEATH OF ONE OF BURNS'S HEROINES – We observe the following announcement in the Edinburgh papers of last week; …

… It may interest the lovers of Scottish poetry to know that Mrs Hay was one

of the special favourites of Burns during his Edinburgh sojourn, and to her are addressed some of the most excellent of his letters in his printed correspondence. This accomplished lady was then unmarried, and is addressed by the poet as "Miss Margaret Chalmers". Next to Mrs Dunlop, Miss Chalmers seems to have stood highest in Burn's estimation, and the unreserved disclosures which he made to her of his feelings and sentiments and private views are the best evidence of the entire confidence which he reposed in her admirable good sense, taste, and judgement."

The obituary goes on to relate a tale of Burns and his knowledge of French.

"Mrs Hay used to relate an amusing anecdote, which we give in the words of Mr Campbell, the poet. 'One of his friends (Mrs Hay, then Miss Chalmers) carried him into the company of a French lady, and remarked with surprise that he attempted to converse with her in her own tongue. Their French however, was mutually unintelligible. As far as Burns could make himself understood, he unfortunately offended the foreign lady. He meant to tell her that she was a charming person and delightful in conversation, but expressed himself so as to appear to her to mean that she was fond of speaking; to which the Gallic dame indignantly replied, that it was quite common for poets to be impertinent as for women to be loquacious.'"

It is likely that this was the event that convinced Burns to seek out Louis Cauvin's French school in the High Street.

My Peggy's Charms

My Peggy's face, my Peggy's form,
The frost of hermit Age might warm;
My Peggy's worth, my Peggy's mind,
Might charm the first of human kind.
I love my Peggy's angel air,
Her face so truly heavenly fair,
Her native grace, so void of art,
But I adore my Peggy's heart.

The lily's hue, the rose's dye,
The kindling lustre of an eye;
Who but owns their magic sway!
Who but knows they all decay!
The tender thrill, the pitying tear,
The generous purpose nobly dear,
The gentle look that Rage disarms,
These are all Immortal charms.

After Edinburgh

Now that he had received his money from William Creech, there was no reason to stay on in Edinburgh and Burns was already making plans for a new chapter in his life.

Jean Armour was pregnant again and her father had thrown her out. Burns left Edinburgh and arrived in Mauchline on 23rd February 1788, where he had found a room for Jean.

He then rented a new farm, Ellisland, near Dumfries, on the 18th March 1788. His landlord was his friend Patrick Miller of Dalswinton; the farm needed a lot of work to make it habitable and it wasn't until the summer of 1789 that Jean and son Robert were able to join him.

In the intervening period, around April 1778, Robert and Jean were married in the offices of Gavin Hamilton in Mauchline.

Above: Ellisland

Ellisland became an almost disastrous enterprise. The land was poor and unprofitable. Burns had already been thinking about a position in the Excise, having written in January to the Earl of Glencairn asking him to use his influence to secure such a post. Burns also wrote to Robert Graham of Fintry, a commissioner in the Excise who he had first met while on his Highland tour at Athole House.

His determination paid off and, after completing his training, he started with the Excise in September 1789. He was no longer shackled by the responsibilities of owning and struggling to make a farm work and duly auctioned off all of the farm equipment. Three years after moving into Ellisland, the family moved to a small flat in Bank Street, Dumfries. With promotion in the Excise, he would be able to support himself and his family.

Here, Burns could work on his musical contributions to James Johnston's *Scots Musical Museum* and George Thomson's *A Select Collection of Original Scottish Airs for the Voice*. Burns looked upon this musical work of preserving songs and tunes for the nation's heritage, a duty of responsibility, for which he could take no money. He contributed hundreds of songs to the collections.

Burns had been made a Burgess of Dumfries 4 years earlier while on a visit to the town, and now he was a resident, playing a full part in town life. He enrolled in the Dumfries Volunteers, was involved with his local Masonic lodge, becoming senior warden, and regularly attended the town's new Theatre Royal.

In 1793, the family, now comprising Jean and children Elizabeth Riddel, William Nicol, Francis Wallace, Robert, and Burns' child with Anna Park, Elizabeth, moved to the house in what is now Burns Street.

Robert Burns died on 26th July 1796, aged 37, and is buried in the Robert Burns Mausoleum in St Michael's Churchyard in Dumfries.

Today, more than 200 years after his death, the work of Robert Burns continues to influence aspects of culture, music and writing, not only in Scotland, but around the globe. His birthday, 25th January, is celebrated worldwide, with thousands of Burns Suppers taking place to celebrate and remember the very extraordinary man who was Robert Burns.

Burns Mausoleum
St Michael's Churchyard
St Michael Street
Dumfries
DG1 2QF
01387 253849

Right: Burns Mausoleum, Dumfries

My Luve is like a Red, Red Rose

O my Luve's like a red, red rose,
That's newly sprung in June:
O my Luve's like the melodie,
That's sweetly play'd in tune.

As fair art thou, my bonie lass,
So deep in luve am I;
And I will luve thee still, my dear,
Till a' the seas gang dry.

Till a' the seas gang dry, my dear,
And the rocks melt wi' the sun;
And I will luve thee still, my dear,
While the sands o' life shall run.

And fare-thee-weel, my only Luve!
And fare-thee-weel, a while!
And I will come again, my Luve,
Tho' 'twere ten thousand mile!

Appendix:

The Shaw Burns – Investigating a Painting

n July 2011, at a provincial saleroom in the south of England, an art enthusiast bought a painting catalogued as AFTER ALEXANDER NASMYTH (1758–1840) PORTRAIT OF ROBBIE BURNS. It was exceptionally dirty, thick with dust and typical of a painting that might have lain for many years, undisturbed and forgotten, possibly to be sold off with the rest of a house clearance. As it turned out, the dust was mostly surface dirt, so the painting did not need much cleaning.

It looked generally the right age, it looked undamaged, and even though there were hundreds of portraits painted after Burns died in 1796 and beyond, there was something about this particular one that was interesting, so he bought it.

The new owner showed the paining to Jeff Applin, an experienced antique dealer, wo pointed out that the glass was rolled leaded glass and the nails hand-made. These facts suggested a date in the last quarter of the eighteenth century, because after this 'cut' nails were beginning to be manufactured with rectangular bodies and a rectangular head.

David Mackie, an established expert on Sir Henry Raeburn and Scottish artists of the 18th century, was contacted and he became involved in the investigation. Was the painting actually by Nasmyth, we wondered?

The four-part strainer was finely made with dovetail joints at each corner. Alexander Nasmyth is known to have had a workshop section in his studio at York Place and could possibly have made the strainer himself. More interesting still was the fact that although the strainer is identical to those on the Edinburgh and London versions of the iconic Nasmyth portrait, to date it hasn't been possible to examine the rear of the Glasgow painting. Inscribed on the rear of the strainer was the word 'Shaw'.

The only Shaw who can be identified with a Burns connection is Sir James Shaw, Kilmarnock-born and a London politician, who was a major benefactor to the Burns family after the death of Robert. Stephen Conrad, an art historian, informed the painting's new owner that the name 'Shaw' may well refer to Sir James Shaw, who rose so quickly in London society, from his poor roots in Kilmarnock, that he was elected Lord Mayor of London in 1805.

After the surface dirt and dust were gently cleaned off, the owner sensibly decided to take the picture to a professional conservator where a light cleaning was carried out.

The very good quality frame – with French influence in its design – holds the portrait, again using hand-made nails. When the portrait was first removed from this a label was found attached to the rebate, but it was dirty and fragile. Jane McAusland, a renowned paper conservator, carefully removed the label, the wording on which is made up from three different styles of typeface. This print technology was not available before the late 1700's. The final line on the label clearly stated that the frame was manufactured in Edinburgh, but as the label was damaged efforts continue to be made to identify the maker.

David Mackie's 2-year study of the work culminated in his confirmation that, in his opinion, the painting was indeed painted by Alexander Nasmyth, and it was during this period that the picture was examined both by infrared and X-ray techniques. The X-ray showed that the painting was original to the canvas and that the preparatory work on the canvas was exactly as Nasmyth would have carried it out, with a one-inch brush on the sky background, using the same type of vertical brushstrokes. The Infrared showed a preparatory pencil drawing on the canvas.

Mackie based his authentication on an exhaustive examination of all aspects of the work and concluded that "I believe it is a Nasmyth. I make that judgement purely based on its style. It is in very good condition and is a really charming little picture." He examined and compared this portrait with the original in Edinburgh, and the London and Glasgow versions.

Given the known style of Nasmyth's portraits of Burns, the Shaw image is remarkably similar to the original showing his chin and jawline as sharp and distinctive, perhaps somewhat effeminate. During the publication of the *Edinburgh Edition*, as the copperplate for the frontispiece engraving of Burns (based on the Nasmyth image) wore down with use, Burns sat several times for the engraver Beugo, as he repaired the plate and re-engraved Burns' image. But in doing so Burns' features, particularly his jawline, gradually became squarer, more masculine, becoming more like the earlier Taylor images that were to emerge several years later.

In 1787–1800, this would have been quite an expensive painting. A high-quality contemporary gilded frame, with expensive rolled glass, would have been destined for someone of substantial means. This wasn't a painting that would have been sitting in a workshop waiting for a buyer, and it is undoubtedly the high quality of all aspects of the painting that has ensured its survival, in remarkable condition, for some 225 years.

Imogen Gibbon, Senior Curator and Deputy Director of the Scottish National Portrait Gallery, said, "This is a very interesting discovery. I would say often people approach museums and galleries with what they think is a new portrait of Burns, but often they date from the 20th or late 19th century, but this appears to be an exception."

David Mackie is the acknowledged expert on the work of Sir Henry Raeburn and is currently completing the definitive study of Raeburn's paintings. Works by Raeburn are now recognised by their Mackie Number.

Jane McAusland, is a Conservator of Fine Art on Paper. At the age of 19 she began what she termed her 10-year apprenticeship with Craddock & Barnard in London, before setting up her own studio. Jane is a world-renowned conservator and a Fellow of the International Institute for Conservation of Historic and Artistic Works. She is an adviser to the auction houses Christie's and Sotheby's, the Henry Moore Foundation and the Royal Academy. Jane has worked extensively for the Natural History Museum and Her Majesty the Queen's Collection in the Royal Library in Windsor Castle.

Jess Applin, of Cambridge, is a highly respected antique dealer (now retired) and member of the British Association of Antique Dealers.

Stephen Conrad, Art Historian, Researcher and Consultant, is based in London.

Opposite: Robert Burns by Alexander Nasmyth
Canvas Size: 16×12 in (41×30.5 cm)
On its original 4-part, finely made strainer and unlined canvas; 'Shaw B604', written in pencil on the strainer.

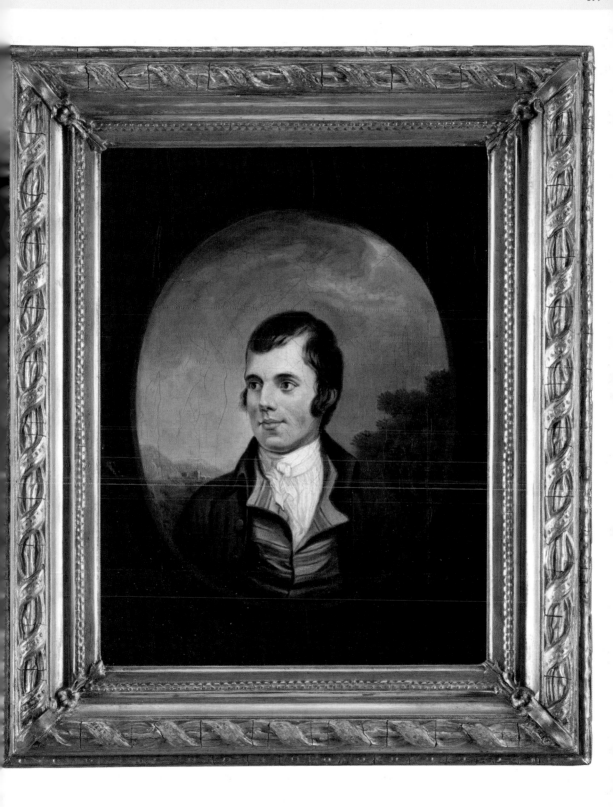

Bibliography by publication date

The Trial of William Brodie and George Smith
William Creech, for and by the author, 1788.

The Trial of William Brodie
Aneas Morison. Charles Elliot, Edinburgh, 1788.

Walker's Hibernian Magazine, a Compendium of Entertaining Knowledge
Various c1790.

Edinburgh Fugitive Pieces
William Creech. Creech, Edinburgh & Cadell, London, 1791.

Aitchison's Edinburgh Directory 1793–1794
Thomas Aithchison. Wilson 1793.

The Thespian Dictionary
Published by T. Hurst. 1802.

Walks in Edinburgh
Robert Chambers. Hunter & Smith, 1825.

A Winter with Robert Burns
Can-Kil. Canongate Kilwinning, 1846.

The Works of Robert Burns
John Lockhart. Leavitt & Trow, New York, 1849.

Edinburgh Merchants and Merchandise in Old Times
Robert Chambers. 1859.

History of the Violin
William Sandy, 1864.

Notes on Old Edinburgh
Isabella Bird. Edmonston & Douglas, 1869.

Original Portraits and Caricature Etchings. Volumes 1 & 2
John Kay. 1877.

Reminiscences of Old Edinburgh. Vols I & II
Daniel Wilson. Douglas Edinburgh. 1879.

The Life and Works of Robert Burns: critical and analytical edition
P. Hately Waddell. David Wilson Glasgow. 1881.

Cassell's Old and New Edinburgh, Its History, Its People an Its Places
Volumes I, II, III. James Grant. Cassell, Petter & Galpin, 1882.

Kay's Edinburgh Portraits. Vols I & II
James Patterson. Hamilton & Adams, London, 1885.

Memorials of Edinburgh in the Olden Time
Daniel Wilson. Grange Publishing Works, 1886.

Annals of the Edinburgh Stage
Dibdin, J.C.R. Cameron, Edinburgh, 1888.

History of Lodge Canongate Kilwinning No.2
Allan MacKenzie. Printed for the Lodge, 1888.

St Giles', Edinburgh. Church, College and Cathedral
J. Cameron Lees. Chambers. 1889.

The Book of Robert Burns
Reverend Charles Rodgers. 1890.

Ancient Old Edinburgh and Some of the Worthies Who Walked its Streets
Alison Hay Dunlop. R&H Sommerville, Stockbridge. 1890.

The Works of Burns Vols I–V
ed. Charles Annandale. Blackie & Sons, c1890.

Literary Landmarks of Edinburgh
Laurence Hutton. Harper & Brothers New York. 1891.

The Book of Robert Burns
Reverend Charles Rodgers & Reverend J.C. Higgins. Grampian Club, 1891.

Slum Life in Edinburgh T.B.M. James Thin, Edinburgh. 1891.

Burns' "Chloris" A Reminiscence
John Adams M.D. Morison Brothers Glasgow. 1883.

Memorable Edinburgh Houses
Wilmot Harrison. Oliphant Anderson & Ferrier. 1893.

New Lights on Old Edinburgh
John Reid. David Douglas Edinburgh. 1894.

The Book of Old Edinburgh. A Handbook to the International Exhibition 1886
John Charles Dunlop & Alison Hay Dunlop. Charles Scibner's Sons, New York. 1896.

The Life and Works of Robert Burns
Robert Chambers. Vol II. W.R. Chambers, 1896.

John Knox and the Town Council of Edinburgh
Robert Miller. Andrew Elliot, Edinburgh. 1898.

Old Edinburgh. Vols I & II
Frederick W. Watkeys. L.C. Page & Co. Boston. 1898.

Literary Life of Edinburgh
A.H. Moncur-Sime. James Clark & Co. London. 1898.

Saint Cecilia's Hall in The Niddrie Wynd
David Fraser Harris. Oliphant Anderson & Ferrier 1899.

Letters and Memoirs of Her Own Life
Mrs Alison Rutherfurd or Cockburn. Douglas, 1900.

Burns Centenary 21st July 1896, The Demonstration at Dumfries
3rd edition, 1902.

Edinburgh Life in the Eighteenth Century
Published by William Brown Edinburgh. 1907.

Register of Marriages for the Parish Church of Edinburgh. 1701–1750
Henry Paton. James Skinner & Co. 1908.

Poems Chiefly in the Scottish Dialect
Robert Burns. Facsimile. Wilson. Kilmarnock, 1909.

The Story of the Edinburgh Burns Relics
Robert Duncan. Andrew Elliot, Edinburgh. 1910.

James Nasmyth: Engineer. An Autobiography
ed. Samuel Smiles. John Murray. London, 1912.

History of the Old Greyfriars Church Edinburgh
William Bryce. Morrison & Gibb. 1912.

Illustrated Guide to St Giles" Cathdral, Edinburgh
Visitor Guide by William Meikle. 1920.

Who's Who in Burns
John D. Ross. Eneas Mackay, Stirling. 1927.

The Letters of Robert Burns
Brimley Johnson. 1928.

Robert Burns as a Volunteer
William Will. William Smith & Sons, Aberdeen, 1928.

A Burns Handbook
John D. Ross. Eneas Mackay, Stirling, 1931.

Burns and His Poetry
H.A. Kellow. Geo. G. Harrap & Co. London, 1935.

Robert Burns, His Life and Tradition in Words and Sound
Ian Nimmo. Record Books, 1965.

The London Stage 1774–1776
G.W. Stone. Southern Illinois University Press, 1968.

Robert Burns' Commonplace Book 1783–85
ed. Raymond Lamont Brown. S.R. Publishers, 1969.

Poems Chiefly in the Scottish Dialect
Robert Burns. Scolar Press. Facsimile, 1971.

Music and Society in Lowland Scotland in the 18th Century
David Johnson. Oxford University Press, 1972.

Balloon Tytler by Sir James Fergusson of Kilkerran, London, 1972.

Literary and Artistic Landmarks of Edinburgh
Andrew Peacock. The Albyn Press, 1973.

An Introduction to Lodge Canongate Kilwinning
W.B. Harvey, 1982.

The Complete Letters of Robert Burns
James A. Mackay. Alloway Publishing, 1987.

Burns: Authentic Likenesses
by Basil Skinner. Alloway Publishing, 1990.

The Edinburgh Graveyard Guide
Michael Turnbull. Saint Andrew Press, 1991.

A Biography of Robert Burns
James McKay. Mainstream, 1992.

Robert Burns
Ian Grimble. Lomond Books, 1994.

Playing For Scotland: History of the Scottish Stage
Donald Campbell, Mercat Press. 1996.

Genealogical Charts of the Family of Robert Burns
Peter J. Westwood. A Burns Federation Production. 1997.

A Walk on The Southside in the Footsteps of Robert Burns
John G. Gray and Charles J. Smith. Southside Museum and Gallery, Edinburgh. 1998.

Burns Country
David Carroll. Sutton Publishing Ltd, 1999.

Garrick
Ian McIntyre. Allen Lane, 1999.

On the Trail of Robert Burns
John Cairney. Luath Press Ltd, 2000.

Theatre in Belfast. 1736–1800
John C. Greene. Lehigh University Press. 2000.

Jean Armour, My Life and Times with Robert Burns
Peter J. Westwood. Creedon Publications. 2001.

Pictures in the Garrick Club
Geoffrey Ashton. Unicorn Press. 2002.

Robert Burns, The Tinder Heart
Hugh Douglas. Sutton Publishing, 2002.

The Canongate Burns
ed. Andrew Noble & Patrick Scott Hogg. Canongate. 2003.

Robert Burns, The Lassies
George Scott Wilkie. Neil Wilson Publishing Ltd. 2004.

Scottish Emigration to Colonial America 1607–1875
David Dobson. University of Georgia Press. 2004.

St Patrick's Edinburgh, 150 Years
Michael Henesy. C.Sr.R. 2006.

181 Old Calton Burial Ground
Edinburgh City Council, Survey of Gardens and Designed
Landscapes. July 2007.

The Complete Songs of Robert Burns
Linn Records. 2007.

*The Haunted North: Paranormal Tales from Aberdeen and the
North East*
Graeme Milne. Cauliay Publishing and Distribution. 2008.

The Theatre Royal: Entertaining a Nation
Graeme Smith. Glasgow Publications, 2008.

The Luath Robert Burns Companion
John Cairney. Luath Press, 2008.

The Bard, Robert Burns, a Biography
Robert Crawford. Jonathan Cape, London, 2009.

Robert Burns, The Patriot Bard
Patrick Scott Hogg. Mainstream, 2009.

Robert Burns and the Hellish Legion
John Burnett. National Museums of Scotland, 2009.

Robert Burns, A Life
Ian McIntyre. Constable. 2009.

Fickle Man, Robert Burns in the 21st Century
Johnny Rodger & Gerard Carruthers. Sandstone Press,
Scotland, 2009.

Robert Burns in Your Pocket Waverley Books. 2012.

The Robert Burns Diaries Fred MacKenzie & Robert Pitt Kelly.
Corporate Merchandising. 1998–2012.

Maurice Lindsay's The Burns Encyclopaedia 4th Edition David
Purdie, Kirsteen McCue and Gerard Carruthers. Robert Hale.
London. 2013.

Dictionary of National Biography Oxford University Press.

*Biographical Dictionary of Actors, Actresses and
Musicians, 1660–1800* Philip Highfill. et al.

Williamson's Edinburgh Directories Various 1784–1792. Peter
Williamson. Denovan.

Chronological List of Royal Company of Scottish Archers
Andrew Duncan.

The Edinburgh Literary Journal, Jan–Jun 1831 Constable & Co,
Edinburgh.

Regent Road, Calton Old Burial Ground and Monuments
Historic Scotland, Edinburgh City Council.

The Writer's Museum Edinburgh Official Handbook.

Online Resources

Robert Burns

www.burnsc21.glasgow.ac.uk, Editing Robert Burns for the 21st Century. Blogs, podcasts, video, and more from the Centre for Robert Burns Studies.

www.burnsmuseum.org.uk, the official website of the Robert Burns Birthplace Museum in Alloway.

www.robertburns.org, the website of Burns Country.

www.rbwf.org.uk, the Robert Burns World Federation

Masonic Connections

www.grandlodgescotland.com, information and resources for Scottish Lodges.

www.lck2.co.uk, the website of Lodge Canongate Kilwinning No. 2.

www.lodge48.webs.com, The Lodge of Edinburgh St Andrew No.48.

Historical Books

www.gutenberg.org, Project Gutenberg, an American site offering free books where their copyright has expired, and information on thousands of others.

www.openlibrary.org, 'the world's classic literature at your fingertips.'

Reference

www.oxforddnb.com, The Oxford Dictionary of National Biography is a record of men and women who have shaped British history.

www.britannica.com, *Encyclopaedia Britannica* online.

www.probertencyclopaedia.com, a fully searchable encyclopaedia and English dictionary.

www.britishnewspaperarchive.co.uk, digitised and searchable pages of historical British newspapers.

General

www.scotland.org, Scottish Government Gateway.

www.royalmile.com, information on the history and area surrounding the Royal Mile.

www.electricscotland.com, information on aspects of Scottish life and culture.

www.gravestonephotos.com, an international directory of grave monuments.

Museums and Libraries

www.nationalgalleries.org, the website of the National Galleries of Scotland, with links to galleries and events.

www.nls.uk, the website of the National Library of Scotland, with details of digital resources.

www.maps.nls.uk, resource of the National Library to access and view over 48,000 maps as high-resolution, colour, zoomable images.

www.capitalcollections.org.uk, the image library for the collections of Edinburgh Libraries and Museums and Galleries.

www.glasgowlife.org.uk/libraries, with link to Glasgow's Mitchell Library. Housed in the Burns Room, the Robert Burns Collection of over five thousand items is believed to be one of the largest collections in the world.

www.canmore.rcahms.gov.uk, National collection of photographs, drawings, manuscripts and books relating to Scotland's buildings, archaeology and industry.

Image credits

All illustrations copyright © Dave Alexander unless otherwise stated

All photographs copyright © Jerry Brannigan unless otherwise stated

p.8 *Birthplace of Burns*. English Illustrated Magazine. 1887. Engraving by Hedley Fitton

p.9 Title page, *Poems Chiefly in the Scottish Dialect* from facsimile edition. 1909

p.11 Map of Isthmus of Panama. Copyright © Volina, courtesy of www.shutterstock.com

p.11 *A New Map of the Isthmus of Darien in America, The Bay of Panama, The Gulph of Vallona or St. Michael, with its Islands and Countries Adjacent*. Public domain, courtesy of en.wikipedia.org

p.12 *A Plan of the Harbour and parts adjacent, where the Scotch Company were settled on the Isthmus of Darien*. Taken from *The Darien Papers*, Thomas Constable, 1849

p.13 Image of John Wilson's Printing Press, The Dick Institute. Reproduced by permission of East Ayrshire Leisure, East Ayrshire Council

p.15 *Leith Harbour about 1700*. Engraving taken from *Old and New Edinburgh*, James Grant, Cassell, Petter, Galpin & Co., 1882

p.17 *Inauguration of Robert Burns as Poet Laureate of Canongate Kilwinning, No.2, 1ˢᵗ March 1787* By William Stewart Watson. 1846. Reproduced by kind permission of The Grand Lodge Of Scotland

p.18 *The Inauguration of Robert Burns as Poet Laureate of the Lodge* by William Stewart Watson, 1846. Oil on Canvas. Acc. No. PG946. NGS

p.23 *Robert Burns, Red Rose* Painted 2013. Reproduced by kind permission of Gordon Irving, Artist. www.popportraits.net

p.23 *Robert Burns, A Forensic Reconstruction* 2013. Reproduced by kind permission of Rab Wilson, Professor Caroline Wilkinson, Dundee University and The Hunter Foundation

p.25 Mrs Agnes McLehose, *Clarinda* 1759–1841. 1788. John Miers. Ink on plaster. Acc. No. PG567. NGS

p.25 *Robert Burns, 1759–1796. Poet*. Alexander Reid. 1795/6. Miniature, watercolour on ivory. Acc. No. PG341. NGS

p.26 *Robert Burns, 1759–1796. Poet*. 1787. Alexander Nasmyth. Oil on canvas. Acc. No. PG1063. NGS

p.27 *Robert Burns, 1759 1796. Poet*. 1801. John Beugo. Line engraving on paper. Acc. No. Sp.IV 29.13. NGS

p.29 *Robert Burns*. c.1828. John Flaxman. Marble. Scottish National Portrait Gallery. Image by Kim Traynor, Photographer. creativecommons.org

p.32 *Robert Burns ('The Shaw Burns')*. Alexander Nasmyth. Oil on Canvas. 1800/10. Image by permission of Jerry Brannigan

p.36 Kirkwood Map of 1819, St James Square section. Reproduced by permission of the National Library Of Scotland

p.37 St James Square and Surrounding Area, (1956). Reproduced by arrangement with The Scotsman Publications

p.51 *Siddons, Sutherland, Woods of Theatre Royal Edinburgh* Drawing by John Kay. 1784. Print from *A Series of Original Portraits and Caricature Etchings by the late John Kay*. Hugh Paton, 1838

p.52 Playbill for *Rob Roy*, performed at Theatre Royal, Edinburgh, March 11ᵗʰ 1829

p.64 *The Cotter's Saturday Night*. Engraving from the original drawing by David Allan

p.81 Fergusson's Grave, Canongate Kirkyard. Reproduced by kind permission of Kim Traynor, Photographer. creativecommons.org

pp.86–8 Interiors, Lodge Canongate Kilwinning No. 2. Photographs by Jerry Brannigan. Reproduced with kind permission of The Royal Order of Scotland

p.101 *Robert Burns, 1759–1796. Poet*. 1786/87. Peter Taylor. Oil on board. Acc. No. PG1085. NGS

p.107 Robert Burns statue, Camperdown, Australia: Civic Centre restoration. Reproduced by kind permission of Graeme Saunders; Courtesy of Monument Australia. www.monumentaustralia.org.au

p.111 Creech's Land. Engraving taken from *Old and New Edinburgh*, Cassell, Petter Galpin and Company, 1880

p.120 Anchor Close. Copyright © StockCube, courtesy of www.shutterstock.com

p.122 *William Smellie printer and Andrew Bell engraver* Drawing by John Kay. 1784. Print from *A Series of Original Portraits and Caricature Etchings by the late John Kay*. Hugh Paton, 1838

p.124 St Giles' Cathedral. Copyright © Heartland Arts, courtesy of www.shutterstock.com

p.126 'The Robert Burns Memorial Window'. Reproduced with kind permission of Leifur Breidfjörd, Stained Glass Artist. Photograph by Leifur Breidfjörd, www.breidfjord.com

p.131 Signage, Deacon Brodie's Tavern. Image by kind permission of Kim Traynor, Photographer. www.creativecommons.org

p.133 *A Sleepy Congregation*, John Kay. Print from *A Series of Original Portraits and Caricature Etchings* by the late John Kay. Hugh Paton, 1838

p.139 *James Bruce, Esq of Kinnaird and Peter Williamson*. John Kay. Print from *A Series of Original Portraits and Caricature Etchings* by the late John Kay. Hugh Paton, 1838

p.145 Lady Stair's Close. Engraving taken from *Old and New Edinburgh*, Cassell, Petter Galpin and Company, 1880

p.159 Holyrood Palace. Image taken from *Souvenir of Scotland: Its Cities, Lakes and Mountains*. T Nelson and Sons, 1892

p.159 Lord and Lady Douglas. Images taken from *The Douglas Cause*, A. Francis Steuart (editor). William Hodge and Company, 1909

p.161 *The Meeting of Robert Burns and Sir Walter Scott at Sciennes Hill House*, by Charles Martin Hardie. 1893. Oil on Canvas. Reproduced with kind permission of The Abbotsford Trust, Abbotsford

p.162 Abbotsford House. Copyright © Jule_Berlin, courtesy of www.shutterstock.com

p.217 *Jane Maxwell, Duchess of Gordon* by William Skeoch Cumming, painted 1897. Reproduced with the kind permission of The Gordon Highlanders Museum

p.219 *The House on Kinrara Estate*. Reproduced with kind permission of David Medcalf, Photographer

p.236 Clarinda's House, General's Entry; Room in Clarinda's House, General's Entry. Engravings taken from *Old and New Edinburgh*, Cassell, Petter Galpin and Company, 1880

p.255 *Ellisland*, from *The Works of Burns Vol I.* 1887

Selected engravings, taken from *The National Burns*, by Reverend George Gilfillan. William Mackenzie, 1878

Map images reproduced by arrangement with RH Publications, MAPS IN MINUTES copyright © 2014.

The illustrations in this book, by David Alexander were based on references from the following sources:

Portraits by Sir Henry Raeburn, James L. Caw, 1909: *Sir Henry Raeburn, R.A. – His Life and Works*, James Greig, 1911; *Sir Henry Raeburn*, W.E. Henley, 1890; *Portraits by Sir Henry Raeburn*, Andrew Elliot, 1907; *Sir Henry Raeburn*, Sir Walter Armstrong, 1901; *Scottish Painting Past and Present*, James L. Caw, 1908; *Masterpieces*, James L. Caw, 1908; *Catalogue of Engraved British Portraits*, H.M. O'Donoghue, 1908; *British Mezzotint Portraits*, J.C. Smith, 1884; *History of Silhouettes*, F. Neville Jackson, 1911; *Portraits in Stipple and Mezzotint*, David H. Peffers, 1901; *The Scots Magazine*, 1774 and 1817; *The Land of Burns*, Blackie and Son, 1840; *Cassell's Old and New Edinburgh: It's History, It's People, and It's Places*, James Grant, 1882; *George Thompson, The Friend of Burns*, J.C. Hadden, 1897; *Memorial Catalogue of the 1896 Burns Exhibition*; *The Heroines of Burns*,1906; *Burns Rare Print Collection*, S. Eaton, 1900; *Burns in Art*, Shelley, 1894; *Memorials of Edinburgh in Olden Time*, D. Wilson, 1907; *The Connoisseur*, 1901; *London Illustrated News*, 1844; *A Series of Original Portraits and Caricature Etchings*, John Kay, 1837-8; *Pictures and Portraits of the Life and Land of R. Burns*, Alan Cunningham, 1840; *Sir Walter Scott's Friends*, Florence McCunn, 1910; *Annals of the Edinburgh Stage*, J.C. Dibdin, 1888; *The Life of Robert Burns*, F.B. Snyder, 1932; *Burns Poetical Works*, William Gunnyon, 1893.

Illustrations based on sketches from *Inauguration of Robert Burns as Poet Laureate at the Lodge Cannongate Kilwinning, Edinburgh, in 1787* by William Stewart Watson, 1846.

David Alexander thanks: Voltaire and Rousseau Antiquarian Books, Glasgow; Great Western Auctions, Glasgow; Grosvenor Prints, London; Dr. Ronnie Scott; Mr. David Black, Mr. Alex Gilchrist; Mr. Ronnie Ferguson and Mr. Gordon Will, for valuable assistance and access to material.

Auld Lang Syne

For auld lang syne, my dear,
For auld lang syne.
We'll tak a cup o' kindness yet,
For auld lang syne.

Should auld acquaintance be forgot,
And never brought to mind?
Should auld acquaintance be forgot,
And auld lang syne?

And surely ye'll be your pint stoup,
And surely I'll be mine;
And we'll tak a cup o' kindness yet,
For auld lang syne.

We twa hae run about the braes,
And pou'd the gowans fine;
But we've wander'd mony a weary fit,
Sin' auld lang syne.

We twa hae paidl'd in the burn,
Frae morning sun till dine;
But seas between us braid hae roar'd
Sin' auld lang syne.

And there's a hand, my trusty fiere!
And gie's a hand o' thine!
And we'll tak a right gude-willie waught,
For auld lang syne.

Burns Statue, Dumfries by Amelia Hill

Engraving by W. Roffe